Dis

COMICS

Shire Publications Ltd

CONTENTS

Introduction: The Editor's Chat 3
Ally Sloper: Side-splitting, Sentimental and Serious! 4
Comic Cuts: One Hundred Laughs for One Half-penny! 7
The Big Budget: Three Papers for One Penny 10
Puck: Bright Wings of Colour and Fancy! 14
The Rattler: Twelve Pages! Free Footballs! One Penny! 19
The Dandy: Our Funsters' Wiles Will Bring You Smiles! 23
Famous Funnies: 100 Comics — 10 Cents! 27
Action Comics: It's a Bird! It's a Plane! It's Superman! 49
Eagle: The New National Strip Cartoon Weekly! 54
Pow! For the New Breed of Comic Fans! 57
British Comics 1960-1980 60
British Comics since 1980 64
Index 71

British Library Cataloguing in Publication Data: Gifford, Denis. 1927- Discovering Comics.—Second edition—(Discovering series, 177). 1. British comics, history. I. Title. 741.5941. ISBN 0-7478-0108-8

Cover: Detail of 'Happy Days'. See page 41 for illustration.

For Pandy — and in memory of John R. Turner

Copyright © 1971 and 1991 by Denis Gifford. First published 1971. Second edition 1991. Number 117 in the Discovering series. ISBN 0 7478 0108 8.

Printed in Great Britain by C. I. Thomas & Sons (Haverfordwest) Ltd, Press Buildings, Merlins Bridge, Haverfordwest, Dyfed SA61 1XF.

INTRODUCTION: THE EDITOR'S CHAT!

1. Your Editor: Mr. Clarence C. Cutts of 'Comic Cuts', 31st October, 1931.

"Hello, chums!"

No self-respecting children's comic was ever published that did not have its Editor's Chat, so it would not seem unreasonable for this first book about them to have one, too.

Increasingly the comic paper is being collected, catalogued, examined and exhibited. In France there is a learned society of students and historians of the comic; in America there is an Academy of Comic Book Arts; in Italy more than one serious magazine is devoted to strip cartoon archaeology. Curiously, only Great Britain, where the comic paper was born, takes its comics for what they superficially seem— ephemera to be discarded as soon as read. There have always been collectors of comics, of course, but their motive is nostalgia—a recapturing of a long-lost childhood. Now, increasingly, comics are being rediscovered for their artistic qualities, as well as for their accidental value as social documents. This concise but comprehensive history of the comic concentrates on the comparatively unknown evolution of the British picture paper, while tracing the parallel development of the American newspaper comic supplement and that vehicle of the super-hero, the comic-book.

"Cheerio, chums!"

ALLY SLOPER: SIDE-SPLITTING, SENTIMENTAL AND SERIOUS!

Alexander Sloper, Ally for short, who lived in The Sloperies and looked at life from a Sloperian point of view, has been called the first British comic strip hero. His weekly paper, *Ally Sloper's Half-Holiday,* has been called the first British comic. Both claims are false, and yet both claims are true. There were earlier comic strip heroes in England: H. G. Hine and Albert Smith drew 'Mr. Candle's Rapid Career Upon the Town' in six successive issues of the monthly magazine *The Man in the Moon* (1847). And there were earlier comic papers: James Henderson of Red Lion Square published *Funny Folks* (Plate 2) from 7th December, 1874 ('A Weekly Budget of Funny Pictures, Funny Notes, Funny Jokes, Funny Stories'). But it was undoubtedly the ubiquitous Ally, 'Friend of Man', bulbous-nosed and battered-hatted, that popularised both the comic strip and the comic paper in this country.

Sloper's happy *Half-Holiday* first occurred on Saturday, 3rd May, 1884, ten years after Henderson's pioneering picture paper set the style of the British comic: eight pages in tabloid (half-newspaper) size, front, back, and centre-spread a jumble of jokes in pictures and panels, with pages 2, 3, 6 and 7 set predominantly in tiny text. It was printed black on white, of course; colour would not come in for twenty years. The editor, or 'conductor' as he preferred to call himself, was Gilbert Dalziel, of the well-known firm of engravers, the Dalziel Brothers. They also printed the paper for the actual proprietor, W. J. Sinkins, and within a couple of years had taken over the publication entirely (issuing it from 'The Sloperies', 99 Shoe Lane, London E.C.). Sloper starred in the large cover cartoon drawn by W. G. Baxter, which first appeared in issue number 13 (21st July, 1884), and it is Baxter's version of the ancient Ally that is best remembered today. In fact, there is an earlier, older Sloper belonging to a pre-comic period.

Charles H. Ross, journalist, parodist, novelist, editor and all-round literary gent, was also a cartoonist. On 14th August, 1867 he contributed a full-page funny to the new magazine, *Judy,* begun as a rival to *Punch.* The page was entitled 'Some of the Mysteries of Loan and Discount' and depicted the money-making machinations of a penniless pair, Ikey Mo and Ally Sloper. Soon this terrible twosome were turning up week after week, and within two years Charles Ross was made

4

ally Sloper's Half Holiday

BEING A SELECTION, SIDE-SPLITTING, SENTIMENTAL, AND SERIOUS, FOR THE BENEFIT OF OLD BOYS, YOUNG BOYS, ODD BOYS GENERALLY, AND EVEN GIRLS

Vol. II.—No. 51.　　　　　SATURDAY, APRIL 18, 1888.　　　　　[ONE PENNY.

AN ODE TO SPRING.
"In early Spring THE OLD MAN'S fancy lightly turns to thoughts of love."

Give Sloper Spring, the merry Spring!　　　Birds and flowers of Spring he loves—
To love in Spring his thoughts turn lightly;　　Swallow, daisy, violet, linnet,
Though Mrs. S. don't quite approve,—　　He loves spring-water—yes, he does!—
Scarce judges she Poor Ally rightly.　　　With just a little something in it.

2. *Adult Comic: Ally Sloper's spring holiday, drawn by W. G. Baxter, 18th April, 1885.*

editor of *Judy*. The drawing chores, finally proving too much for even so prolific a person as Ross, were taken over by a French teenager, Isabelle Emily de Tessier, who signed her pages 'Marie Duval'.

Ally Sloper, as depicted by the Ross-Duval partnership, became tremendously popular. The cartoons were collected and reprinted in paperback form, selling at one shilling, complete with a specially-drawn cover and an 'official autobio-

5

graphy'. This 216-page special, published November 1873, can claim to be the world's first comic-book (Plate 1). A number of other Sloper specials were produced during the succeeding decade, and the Ross-Duval strips were reprinted yet again in the pages of the Dalziel *Half-Holiday*, twenty years later. The angular, spiky figures seem awkward and amateurish against the detail of W. G. Baxter's great panels, especially his enormous double-page cartoons which form the full centre-spreads of the Christmas issues.

Every year Dalziel published a double-sized, double-priced special, *Ally Sloper's Christmas Holidays*. These bumper numbers, besides the great picture spread (termed the 'gratis plate'), presented readers with an annual treat in the form of a piece of music, 'specially composed for A. Sloper, Esq., F.O.M.' by such worthies as Leopold Wenzel (Composer and Chef D'Orchestre at the Empire Theatre, Leicester Square) or the Chevalier L. Del Bono (Musical Director at the Royal Aquarium, London). Wenzel's piece for the Christmas of 1892 was entitled 'Tootsie's Serpentine Dance'—Tootsie being the bright young miss of the Sloperies. This establishment by now included not only Mrs. Sloper and The Boy Sloper, but the Hon. Billy, Lord Bobs, Dook Snook, Uncle Boffin, Aunt Geeser, and two ladies of the chorus named Lardi Longsox and Nellie Hikiks!

Sloper's Christmas Holidays were published as extras and not numbered within the *Half-Holiday* series. The actual numbered run was 1,788 issues, from 3rd May, 1884 to 9th September, 1916, but half a dozen years later a new series began, published by The Sloperies Ltd. This run commenced on 5th November, 1922, but dropped Ally's name from the title on 21st April, 1923, becoming simply *Half-Holiday* with number 24. The old man's days were clearly numbered: another 24 weeks and the revival folded at issue 47, dated 29th September, 1923.

But there was life in the old boy yet—in 1948, at the grand old age of 71, Ally Sloper turned up just once more, drawn by T. D. Reid for D. McKenzie, a small publisher of Glasgow. *Ally Sloper,* hopefully labelled 'No. 1', was an eight-page, two-colour comic, priced at 3d. Inside, Tootsie Sloper, now called Tootsy, tried for a film test. 'Next month Tootsy sees the test. Will she be a success?' asked the editor. We shall never know —there was no number two. But in its minor way, this half-size, all-picture *Ally Sloper* made history: for the first time Ally appeared in what we know today as a true comic: a picture paper for children. For in all his original long run, Ally was intended for adults only.

COMIC CUTS: ONE HUNDRED LAUGHS FOR ONE HALF-PENNY!

Comic Cuts, whose constant claim to fame as the first ever British comic paper was as fictitious as its eternal editor, Mr. Clarence C. Cutts himself, was born on 17th May, 1890. Preceding it came, in order of appearance, *Funny Folks* (7th December, 1874), *Scraps* (29th August, 1883), *Ally Sloper's Half-Holiday* (3rd May, 1884), *Illustrated Tid-Bits* (4th October, 1884), *Jack and Jill* (7th March, 1885), *Jack's Journal* (14th May, 1887), *Snacks* (15th June, 1889), and *Laughter* (15th February, 1890). All these were in the now standard tabloid comic format, except for *Laughter,* which tried, unsuccessfully, a half-tabloid format. All were also aimed at the adult market, with the exception of *Jack and Jill*—and this was quickly converted to the accepted adults-only formula after a mere seven weeks of illustrated nursery rhymes and Edward Lear. Although none of these weekly papers cost more than a penny a copy, there were few children of the Victorian era with that amount of money to spend on light reading. Consequently the early comic paper was created to entertain the nineteenth century clerk and artisan, and it is not until after the Great War that the English comic can be held to be a publication primarily for the juvenile market.

Comic Cuts was for many years no exception to this rule: its occasional use of picture stories was invariably labelled 'Something special for the children'. But for all its false claims to fame, one remains unchallenged: 'One hundred laughs for one half-penny!' *Comic Cuts* began the boom in comic papers by introducing a not-so-comic cut of its own: a fifty per cent slice in price. This somewhat sensational move was typical of the paper's publisher, a young man twenty-five years old and a former contributor of articles to James Henderson's magazines, Alfred Harmsworth.

Harmsworth and his brothers had already launched a cut-price weekly magazine modelled on George Newnes' successful publication *Tit-Bits.* This was called *Answers to Correspondents* (12th June, 1888), and inside a year it had quadrupled its initial circulation. Now the Harmsworth boys looked at the success Henderson was having with *Funny Folks* and *Scraps* and so put together their own version, *Comic Cuts.* It was so much like Henderson's papers that it even reprinted strips Henderson himself had reprinted from American magazines more than five years earlier.

The American weekly illustrated magazines, *Judge, Life* (in its pre-photographic news magazine days), and *Harper's Weekly,* were prime sources for most of the early British comics. Cartoons and strips, drawn by such early masters of the form as F. B. Opper, H. M. Howarth, L. M. Glackens, and 'Chip' Bellew, filled the pictorial pages of *Comic Cuts* and company; only *Sloper* remained original—and half of his *Half-Holiday* was culled from the seventies' *Judy*! It was Harmsworth again who initiated a boom in native comic art by advertising in *Cuts* for British contributors. Perhaps Henderson, who claimed full copyright in his transatlantic reprints, exercised his option, forcing Harmsworth into such an expensive quest. At any rate, English strip cartoons shortly began to appear in *Cuts,* signed Roland Hill and Vandyke Browne.

On 5th August, 1891, a series entitled 'Popular Songs Illustrated' appeared in *Comic Cuts,* and for the first time Vandyke Browne dropped his pseudonym and signed himself in full: Tom Browne. He was twenty years old, an ex-apprentice to a Nottingham lithographer, and all set to conquer the world with nib and ink. By the turn of the century, Tom Browne had single-handedly created the British comic, set a style that would stretch into the 1950s, and left comic papers behind him to become even more famous—and popular—in posters, picture postcards, and the world of water-colour.

It was on the front page of Alfred Harmsworth's second venture into comic papers that Tom Browne found his forté *Illustrated Chips* was launched on 26th July, 1890 in a half-tabloid format, but even sixteen pages for a halfpenny could not catch the interest of a public brought up on a diet of Sloper's tabloids. After six issues Harmsworth unfolded his pages and sent *Chips* out in the accepted eight-page format, numbering again from one (6th September, 1890). The revised size met with instant acclaim, and *Chips* joined *Comic Cuts* (Plate 11) in a partnership constant for more than half a century: the companions died together in a publishers' purge on 12th September, 1953, *Cuts* combining with *Knockout* and *Chips* combining with *Film Fun.* (*Chips* was revived in title only as a pull-out centre section to a comic called *Whizzer* on 18th October, 1969. Still running, this makes it the longest-lived comic title in publishing history.)

'Innocents on the River' was the heading for Tom Browne's set of six pictures which filled the upper half of the front page of *Chips* on 16th May, 1896. It featured the slapstick mishaps of two tramps, one fat, the other thin. In the typeset text beneath the pictures they were called Weary Waddles and

8

3. *The King of Comics: heading by Roy Wilson, 1933.*

Tired Timmy. Within a few weeks this pair of tattered tramps had taken over the entire front page where, rechristened 'Weary Willie and Tired Tim', they reigned supreme until the final edition, numbered 2997. Of course, Tom Browne did not draw them all; in fact, he gave them up after a mere five years. But he set the style and the standard, and even Percy Cocking, last and best of many subsequent cartoonists, still drew the tramps and their troubles in the careful, balanced, humanly humorous linework laid down by Tom Browne.

Browne's artwork graces many of the early comics, usually in the large six-panel page-one strips. His magazine work was collected into a series of Christmas paperbacks, *Tom Browne's Annual,* but few of his comic contributions were included. He died in 1910, much too young, but his influence can still be found in the comic papers of today.

4. *Tom Browne Tradition: Weary Willie and Tired Tim still at it in 'Chips', 16th July, 1938; drawn by Percy Cocking.*

9

THE BIG BUDGET: THREE PAPERS FOR A PENNY!

Red Lion Court, Red Lion Square, off Fleet Street the home of the London newspapers, was a hive of the popular publishing industry in the 1890s. Not only James Henderson, publisher of the original British comic papers *Funny Folks* and *Scraps* and the famous juvenile story paper *Our Young Folks' Weekly Budget,* operated here; his neighbours were Trapps, Holmes and Company, publishers of *Funny Cuts.* This comic was edited by Gordon Philip Hood ('The funniest man on earth!'), and was brought out at a halfpenny as a direct rival to Harmsworth's *Comic Cuts.* The first issue was dated 2nd July, 1890, and was made up of the standard run of old American reprints. However, number 16 (15th October) made British comic history by running the first full front-page strip cartoon. This was drawn by Alfred Gray, who had contributed many comic pages to *Judy* magazine. *Funny Cuts* lasted for thirty years, and ran to a total of 1,566 issues.

The comic boom was on. Henderson struck again with *Snap-Shots* (9th August, 1890), just a fortnight after Harmsworth issued his first half-sized *Chips.* Henderson, unable to produce a half-penny paper, doubled his page count instead and offered sixteen pages for a penny. But he could not procure original artwork within his lowered budget, so made do entirely with American reprints. The British Publishing Company, another resident of Red Lion Court, came out with *Skits* on 27th June, 1891, but only ran 23 issues. Next came *The Joker* (18th July, 1891), published by T. Murray Ford, a racy paper with an eye for the current lovelies of the contemporary variety stage. 'Tony Green', the front page hero, had a weekly embarrassing encounter with his frilly cousins. Henderson produced two more reprint papers, *Comic Pictorial Sheet* (29th September, 1891), a vast broadside of blocks, and *Comic Pictorial Nuggets* (7th May, 1892), which became simply *Nuggets* with effect from number 30 (26th November). Two weeks later it introduced a pull-out section of text entitled *Story Nuggets.* This section was later absorbed into the body of paper, which thus became more of a magazine with cartoons and occasional strips until it disappeared in 1906.

The World's Comic (6th July, 1892) was supposedly edited by Grandad Twiggle, but those who knew their Trapps, Holmes and Co. could deduce the hand of G. P. Hood, that 'funniest man in the world', behind the pseudonym. At first, like its companion *Funny Cuts* (with which it ultimately com-

10

LAST WEEK OF HAIR RESTORER COMPETITION.

The Big Budget. 1d

BEGIN THE NEW SERIAL
AT ONCE.

VOL. III. No. 54.   WEEK ENDING SATURDAY, JUNE 25, 1898.   PRICE 1D.

AIRY ALF AND BOUNCING BILLY JOIN THE LOCAL FIRE BRIGADE.

5. *Tom Browne's Heroes: Airy Alf and Bouncing Billy in Pearson's 'The Big Budget', 25th June, 1898.*

bined), this comic was content with the usual run of reprints, but towards the end of its long run, regular characters of English origin were introduced, such as 'Birdie and Napoleon'.

Harmsworth's third venture was *The Wonder* (30th July, 1892), and once again he tried a new format: a four-page folded broadsheet as big as a newspaper: 'Why, it is positively giving you a twopenny paper for a quarter of its value!' Readers failed to agree, and after 27 issues Harmsworth succumbed to his own success and started the paper from number one again, in the standard *Comic Cuts* format. This time as *The Funny Wonder* it caught on, and ran more or less continuously, with slight changes of title and format, to that fatal day in September 1953. It pretended to join forces with *Radio Fun,* but really, like its chums *Cuts* and *Chips,* it died.

George Emmett and Charles Fox, who had made much success in the field of the boys' story paper, tried out a comic on 9th August, 1892, but *Jolly Bits,* as they called it, ran no more than six issues. Henderson returned on 20th February, 1893, with yet another comic, *Varieties.* This bargain offered 32 pages for a penny, sixteen of cartoons, and sixteen of stories—but, as might be expected, they were all reprints. Gilbert Dalziel supplemented Sloper by producing *Larks* (1st

May, 1893), which featured a bunch of bad boys called 'The Ball's Pond Road Banditti'. This front page, nicely sketched by G. Gordon Fraser, may have been the first funny feature to draw regular readership from the children of the family—who would ultimately become the main customers for the comic. *The Champion Comic* (9th January, 1894) made another step in the juvenile direction when it began running 'A Bad Boy's Diary' from 27th July, 1895. Alfred Gray, who had been drawing strips for Trapps, Holmes and Co., was now promoted to the editorship of their new comic *Side-Splitters* (6th August, 1894), but this half-size experiment ran for no more than nine weeks.

Harmsworth next tried a story paper, *The Boys' Home Journal,* but it flopped. After five issues he switched it to conform with the comics craze, and as *The Comic Home Journal* it ran for 488 issues from 11th May, 1895. Subtitled 'The Friday Edition of *Chips*' and supposedly edited by Cornelius Chips himself, this comic did more to establish the regularly recurring strip cartoon character than any of its many predecessors. These began with 'Mr. Chips' Dreams' (drawn by Frank Holland), and continued with 'Mary Jane's Sittywations' and 'The Adventures of Softop when Trying to Make a Bit'. Earlier, *Comic Cuts* had introduced 'The Adventures of Chubb-Lock Holmes' drawn by Jack B. Yeats (18th November, 1893) and 'Comic Cuts Colony' by Frank Wilkinson (10th November, 1894), which appeared sometimes as a picture story, sometimes as a large panel, and sometimes as a series of separate joke cartoons. One of the colonists was 'Smirk the Elephant Detective', a parody on a popular story series of the time, 'Dirk the Dog Detective'. The first regular strip on the cover of *Cuts* featured 'Chokee Bill and Area Sneaker' (27th February, 1897), and burglars, along with tramps such as Willie and Tim, remained popular comic paper characters for many years.

C. Arthur Pearson launched *The Big Budget* on 19th June, 1897, subtitling it, 'Three Papers for a Penny' (Plate 3). This 24-page pennyworth in full tabloid size was separated into three sections. First came eight pages of comic strips and funny stories; next came *The Comrades' Budget,* and finally *The Story Budget,* two eight-page sections of illustrated text. Page one of the comic section was held by Tom Browne, now the uncrowned king of the English comic artists. His adventures of 'Airy Alf and Bouncing Billy' were inspired by his own adventures as a keen cyclist; later they were taken over by 'Yorick', the paper's art editor. 'Doings at Whackington School' was a back page strip that Browne began in number

21—another step in the direction of that up-and-coming juvenile market. Jack B. Yeats drew 'Signor McCoy the Wonderful Circus Horse', the first funny animal in English comics and undoubted ancestor of 'George the Jolly Gee Gee', Roy Wilson's superb frontispiece to *Radio Fun* forty years later (Plate 13).

Outstanding cartoon series introduced under Yorick's art editorship include Frank Holland's 'Startling Stories of Jimmer Squirm and Spooky the Sprat' (1900) and Ernest Wilkinson's 'Doings of Von Puff, Von Eye, Iko Italiano, and Von Sausage the Dog' (1901). The paper itself ran until 1909, considerably longer than its companion, *Dan Leno's Comic Journal*. Despite excellent drawings of that music hall idol by Tom Browne, this comic foundered after 93 issues from 26th February, 1898.

The Halfpenny Comic was published by George Newnes (the *Tit-Bits* man) on 22nd January, 1898, and from number 16 an inside set called 'Those Terrible Twins' moved to the front page: a further blow in the cause of juvenile liberation! *Comic Bits* (19th February, 1898) and *The Monster Comic* (15th March, 1898) had but brief lives, but *Pictorial Comic Life* (2nd July, 1898), a Henderson publication, fared incredibly better, being killed off by the Amalgamated Press after a take-over at the ripe old age of thirty years and 1,543 issues. By then it was printed in colour.

6. *Wilkinson's All Sorts: Von Puff, Von Eye, Iko Italiano, and Von Sausage the Dog, by Ernest Wilkinson. 'The Big Budget' 3rd August, 1901.*

PUCK: BRIGHT WINGS OF COLOUR
AND FANCY

The Coloured Comic (21st May, 1898) published by Trapps, Holmes and Co. and printed by the London Colour Printing Company of Exmoor Street, North Kensington, claimed to be the first British comic printed in four colours (red, blue, yellow and black). In fact it had been preceded by several experimental comics in colour, published 'at great expense' by Alfred Harmsworth. The first British coloured comic was, in fact, the special autumn edition of *Comic Cuts,* number 331, 12th September, 1896. It was a brave failure, much improved upon by the Christmas issue of 5th December, which, like the earlier special, cost twice the usual price—one penny! Later came colour editions of *Funny Wonder* and *Chips,* but it was not until 30th July, 1904, that Harmsworth issued his first regular comic in full colours.

Puck, carefully ignoring the pioneering *Coloured Comic,* claimed to be 'the first number of the first coloured comic' and the editor waxed lyrical to boot: '*Puck* is a new paper. He has come to stay, to gladden your eye with his bright wings of colour and fancy . . .' He stayed, in fact, for 36 years, finally succumbing to amalgamation into *Sunbeam* on 11th May, 1940. At first *Puck* followed the style of the American Sunday newspaper comic sections as a sort of outsize cartoon magazine for the family. Early issues featured full-page cover jokes drawn by Bert Thomas, Fred Bennett and Lawson Wood (later famous for his 'Gran'pop' paintings). However, it was not long before 'Johnny Jones' took over the front page. By Christmas he had encountered the scruffy ruffians of 'Casey Court', who normally sported in a large panel of pranks in *Chips,* and *Puck* could be considered entirely a publication for children (Plate 6).

Other artists were introduced from the 'ha'penny blacks': Jack B. Yeats came over with 'The Strange Adventures of Sandab the Sailor', and Tom Wilkinson contributed 'Professor Radium the Scientific Man' in colour. Their artwork, always good, was even better in *Puck,* which maintained a high standard of cartooning throughout its career. It also introduced the adventure strip to the British comic, with the long-running, globetrotting saga of 'Rob the Rover', as depicted in twelve neat panels a week by Walter Booth. In its later years *Puck* concentrated almost exclusively on adventure strips, but apart from the cinematic style of young Reg Perrott, preferred to stick rigidly to the Walter Booth 'story book' style.

Henderson struck back at his old rival by using Harmsworth's own price-cutting tactics: *Lot-O'-Fun* (17th March, 1906) had a front page in full colour yet cost only a halfpenny! This depicted 'The Frolics of Findem and his Friends', aeronautical autograph hunters who ballooned to the palace of no less a celebrity than the Emperor of Germany! A more durable character was 'Dreamy Daniel', drawn by George Davey. The back page dreams of this hapless tramp soon moved to the front page, where they remained for almost the complete run (1,196 issues) of this long-lived comic. Its success led to Henderson adding colour to his *Comic Life* which, after the two comics had been taken over by Harmsworth's Amalgamated Press (13th March, 1920), turned into a second-rate *Puck*. 'The Jolly Adventures of the Captain, the Cook and the Cabin Boy', drawn by Louis Briault, was a poor page one, and, after an alarming lowering of age-appeal, 'Jolly Fun with Jumbo the Baby Elephant', also by Briault, an even poorer one.

Harmsworth's first halfpenny coloured comic was *Chuckles* (10th January, 1914). This was more slapstick in style than *Puck,* although the standard of drawing was generally higher than its counterparts the 'ha'penny blacks'. These now included *Larks* (7th June, 1902), by Trapps, Holmes, who turned it into *The Best Budget* on 15th March, 1906, and back into *Larks* again on 7th June; *Butterfly* (17th September, 1904), with 'Portland Bill' drawn by a former postcard artist, G. M. Payne; *Smiles* (5th May, 1906), *Picture Fun* (16th February, 1909), and *Merry Thoughts* (5th February, 1910), all by Trapps, Holmes; *Merry and Bright* (22nd October, 1910), a comic which starred a number of music hall artists, including 'The Farcical Adventures of Nellie Wallace' by A. Akerbladh; *The Favourite Comic* (21st January, 1911); *My Funnybone* (4th September, 1911); *The Jester* (27th January, 1912), which introduced 'The Comical Capers of Constable Cuddlecook'; and *The Big Comic,* another from Henderson (17th January, 1914).

'Tiger Tim and the Bruin Boys', perhaps the most famous and best loved of all British comic characters, appeared on the colourful front page of *The Rainbow* (14th February, 1914), as drawn by Julius Stafford Baker, the creator of 'Casey Court' in *Chips* (Plate 7). Already four years old, they first appeared in a coloured comic supplement to Arthur Mee's monthly part-work, *The New Children's Encyclopaedia* (15th February, 1910). And although *Rainbow* finally disappeared on 28th April, 1956, the Bruin Boys still carry on, albeit in a streamlined style closer to the animated cartoon film than

15

7. *Trouble Bruin: Tiger Tim and the Bruin Boys by H. S. Foxwell in 'Rainbow', 1922.*

the very Edwardian original of sixty years ago. Favourite of the several Tiger Tim artists was always Harry Foxwell, who left the Amalgamated Press to renovate the weekly *Teddy Tail* supplement (Plate 10) in the *Daily Mail* (1933). The success of the Bruin Boys prompted the publication of *Tiger Tim's Tales* 1st June, 1919), which became *Tiger Tim's Weekly* (31st January, 1920), and a similar comic designed for girls, *Playbox* 14th February, 1925), which featured the Foxwell-drawn doings of Tiger Tilly and the Hippo Girls.

The newly-discovered market for the nursery comic—which

implied papers designed for children but bought by parents—
was responsible for the several sudden descents in age-appeal
already mentioned, and for the fate of Henderson's *Sparks*
(21st March, 1914), which became *Little Sparks* (22nd May,
1920) once the Amalgamated Press had taken it over. An
A. P. comic which sounded young in intention but was not
in fact was *The Firefly* (20th February, 1915).This, following
the success of *The Funny Wonder* once it had established
Charlie Chaplin as its front page strip star, put Charlie's
brother Syd on its own. To make doubly sure of success, they
used the same cartoonist, Bertie Brown. Unhappily neither
Syd nor *Firefly* had the right appeal, and the paper merged
with *Butterfly* after 111 weeks.

The first half-size comic to succeed was *Playtime* (29th May,
1919), a nursery weekly with lots of colour and an excellent
single-picture cover drawn by Harry Rountree. It finished as a
full tabloid comic and changed its name to *Bo-Peep* (19th
October, 1929). Another unusual comic was *The Sunday Fairy*
(10th May, 1919), a title that proved less than box-office. It
changed to *The Children's Fairy* (1st November, 1920), and
then to *Bubbles* (16th April, 1921), surrendering entirely to the
pressures of comic commerce with 'The Bunty Boys' drawn
by Harry Foxwell. *Chick's Own* (25th September, 1920) and
Tiny Tots (22nd October, 1927) were twin ex-per-i-ments in
hy-phen-a-ted ed-u-ca-tion, featuring 'Ru-pert the Chick' and
'Ti-ny and Tot' respectively. Nicely drawn in big pictures they

8. *Cinema Star: Charlie Chaplin, King of the Kinema, by
Bertie Brown: 'Funny Wonder', 23rd May, 1931.*

created a whole new generation of comic readers. *Sunbeam* (7th October, 1922) and *Jungle Jinks* (8th December, 1923) were standard nursery fare, but *My Favourite* (28th January, 1928) preferred picture serials such as that wonder dog of Wardour Films, 'Strongheart'.

Crackers (23rd February, 1929) and *Sparkler* (20th October, 1934) looked rather different. They were coloured comics produced by the 'black comic' department of the Amalgamated Press. This brought a new look to the 'tuppenny coloureds' of the thirties, as former black-and-white practitioners of slapstick strips found their work appearing in full colour. Some found it constricting, but Roy Wilson, best of all the penny black artists, answered the challenge by surpassing even his previous fine achievements in the sequence of 'new-look' coloured penny comics which had begun with *Jingles* (13th January, 1934). This eight-pager was printed on front and back in red and black, and was an attempt to raise the standard of the slapstick 'blacks'. Wilson drew the doings of 'The Tiddlewink Family' on page one, and followed up with the slightly more seriously-drawn 'Adventures of Jerry, Jenny and Joe' in *Tip Top* (21st April, 1934). This companion comic was printed in black and green, but soon changed the overlay colour to orange. Orange was also the colour chosen for *Golden* (23rd October, 1937), which sported another Wilson cover, 'Lieutenant Daring and Jolly Roger, the Bold Sea Rovers'. Wilson, who was by this time considered the finest artist ever to work in British comics, invariably launched first issues at the Amalgamated Press. He drew 'Jack Sprat and Tubby Tadpole of H.M.S. Hotpot' for *The Jolly Comic* (19th January, 1935), which was printed in blue ink, and his presence was felt behind the excellent if derivative front page of 'Jolly Joe and his Fun Show', drawn by Ray Bailey when *Jolly* burst into two-tone red and black on 18th March, 1939.

It was Wilson who was chosen to draw the front page of the A.P.'s venture into full colour gravure. 'Chimpo's Circus' in *Happy Days* (1st October, 1938) (Pl. 9) is the apex of his art and the apotheosis of British comic style. This excellent but expensive experiment was produced as an answer to Walt Disney's *Mickey Mouse Weekly*, launched on 8th February, 1936, by Odhams Press as the first colour comic to be printed photogravure. It was an instant success, and once the lingo of the reprinted American strips had been toned down, it met with that vital parental approval necessary for any pre-war comic priced at twopence. Disney-originated material apart, it included much good British artwork, ranging from the traditionally Victorian science-fiction strips of H. Stanley

White to the forward-looking costume sagas of **Reg Perrott**. Several of the serial strips, and even Basil Reynolds' 'Skit, Skat and the Captain', were reprinted in America in comicbooks published by Whitman, an unheard-of-tribute to British comic art (Plate 8).

THE RATTLER: TWELVE PAGES! FREE FOOTBALLS! ONE PENNY!

Harmsworth's empire, the Amalgamated Press, was by the twenties England's number one fun factory. It had outlived, outgrown, and outbidded all rivals. Trapps, Holmes had vanished; James Henderson had been taken over; George Newnes had folded his single comic *Merry Moments* (started 12th April, 1919) after 194 issues. Sphinx, a newcomer, closed their *All-Picture Comic* after only sixteen. (It had commenced on 12th March, 1921.)

Then on 23rd September, 1922, came a direct challenge: number one of *The Monster Comic*. The publisher, calling himself the Fleetway Press, was Harold Mansfield. He was an old A.P. man with some years of editorial experience on *Merry and Bright* and *Butterfly,* and he designed his *Monster* in the traditional A.P. image. But what was more important, he produced it to sell at one penny. The A.P. had kept their black 8-page comics at the price of three-halfpence since wartime paper shortages had forced the gradual rise from the original halfpenny. Now they faced competition so keen that they swiftly scaled down their price to conform with Mansfield's *Monster*.

Page one was drawn by Reg Carter, another 'stripper' who had begun as a seaside postcard artist. His choice of characters seemed highly contemporary—'Wireless Willie and Bertie Broadcast'— but basically they were little more than Weary Willie and Tired Tim 'wired for sound'. Fleetway's first venture was a great success, and Mansfield followed up with *The Golden Penny Comic* (14th October, 1922), printed on orange paper. 'The Wonderful Wanderings of Wun Lung, Captain Cuttle's Chinese Cook' was eventually displaced from the front page by an extraordinary strip entitled 'Pot T. Pot and his Pet Patient Piecan'. This tasteless series concerning the escapades of an escaped lunatic was drawn, and crudely so, by youthful H. Louis Diamond, who would shortly become a key figure in independent comic publishing. On a higher level of artistry were the illustrations to such type-set tales as 'Anthony Grex the Human Bloodhound'. These were drawn by Eric R. Parker, considered the finest of all the 'Sexton Blake' illustrators.

The A.P. hit back at Fleetway with *Larks* (29th October, 1927), which like *Chips* was printed on pink paper. Bertie Brown drew 'Dad Walker and his son Wally' on the front page, and inside 'Peggy the Pride of the Force' made an early tribute to Women's Lib. This series had the distinction of being drawn by three members of the same family: Harry Parlett (again a former postcard artist) and his sons Reg and George (both of whom are still drawing for the comics of today).

One week later, Fleetway Press struck again with *The Joker* (5th November, 1927). It was the last straw: Fleetway was bought up. A.P. killed *Golden Penny* early the next year, and *Monster* two years later. *Joker*, however, was kept on, and although it amalgamated with *Chips* on 18th May, 1940, it remains one of the A.P.'s best remembered penny blacks, thanks to its funny front page strip. 'Alfie the Air Tramp and Wagger the Sky Terrier', drawn by John Jukes. So the Fleetway Press was no more, legally; but the old comic strips were reprinted by another small publisher, C. A. Ransom, who christened his compilations *Merry Moments, Sunny Comic, Cheerful Comic, Happy Comic, Tip Top,* and, somewhat inaccurately, *Up-To-Date Comic*!

C. Arthur Pearson now re-entered the comic field with a series of specials published at suitable seasons of the year. There was *The Holiday Comic, The Seaside Comic,* and *The Summer Comic,* followed by *The Christmas Comic* and, in due course, *The Spring Comic.* They were twelve-page colour jobs on the traditional *Puck* pattern, selling at 2d and dating from 1931 to 1939. Pearson's last effort was a 32-page twopenny modelled on *The Knock-Out,* entitled *The Monster* (1939).

The centre of the independent comic industry now moved from London to Bath, where a small outfit allied to the A.B.C. Press, who had the Palace Printing Works in Charlotte Street, set themselves up as Provincial Comics Ltd. Their first attempt was a half-tabloid eight-pager appropriately entitled *The Midget* (5th June, 1931) and selling at a halfpenny. It was drawn in its entirety by one anonymous cartoonist and somewhat illiterately edited by Monty Midge: 'Dear Midgites, How is this for a good ha'pporth?' From the third issue the page count rose to twelve and the price to one penny, and on 12th September came more changes: the pages were unfolded to full tabloid size and the name became *The Merry Midget*. Numbering began from one again. H. Louis Diamond now

9. *Topical Comic: Alfie the Air Tramp celebrates Boat Race Day in 'The Joker', 11th April, 1936; drawn by John L. Jukes.*

came in as front page artist, drawing 'Mickey Midge the Merry Midget'. His work also appeared in *The Sparkler,* a companion paper which had started the same week. This one had the advantage of a front page by Bert Hill, a young Channel Islander whose 'Breezy Moments on Wurzel Farm', drawn in the traditional A.P. comic style, showed promise of a merry maturity to come. Despite stories of a prototype Batman, 'Robin All-Alone; or, The Avenging Bat', *Sparkler* ran but twenty weeks, folding with its companion on 23rd January, 1932.

H. Louis Diamond contributed a quick strip to the back page of the boys' magazine *Rover,* then bobbed up a year later, still in Bath, as Target Publications of Locksbrook Road, Lower Weston. From here there issued on 19th August, 1933 the first number of *The Rattler.* This rather hasty-looking affair on pink paper, despite its Bert Hill cover ('Crazy Kink the Goofy Gangster'), could only have appealed on a bargain basement level: 'Free Footballs! Twelve Pages! One Penny!' However, once the comic's format settled down to the now standard centre-spread style, it caught on. *The Dazzler,* Diamond's second challenger, was launched the following day. It was printed on yellow paper, with both front and back by Hill: 'Charlie Chuckle' and 'Barnacle Ben the Breezy Buccaneer'. Both comics ran 294 issues. A third comic appeared on 31st March, 1934: *The Chuckler* was orange and, after a special sixteen-page debut, reduced to the standard Target twelve—which was four more pages than the regulation

21

10. *Combined Comic: 'Rattler' and 'Chuckler' merge into 12 pages for one penny. Heading by Louis Diamond, Harry Coe by Bert Hill; 28th January, 1939.*

A.P. eight. Hill was again the cover artist with 'Sammy Smile'. Diamond not only named his next comic after his flourishing fun foundry, *Target,* but drew the entire first issue by himself! 'Tom Tip and Tim Top the Tricky Toddlers' were on page one, number one (15th June, 1935), taken over from number two by Bert Hill. *Target* ran to eight pages only, on green paper, and was perhaps the closest in style and standard to an A.P. publication. *Rocket* (26th October, 1935) was unique among all the comics of the period: it contained no type-set stories at all, just eight solid pages of pictures, a total of 125 panels. Best was the back page, 'The Admiral's Log', drawn by E. H. Banger, an excellent cartoonist in the Tom Browne tradition who had come over to Target from the Amalgamated Press. *Sunshine* shone forth from white paper on 16th July, 1938. With this eight-pager, Diamond experimented on layout. He drew a large, dramatic story illustration on the cover, bordering it with 'Larry Laff'. Finally, on 11th February, 1939, Target Publications made a last, desperate throw. They launched *The Bouncer*: sixteen pink pages for a penny! Diamond added a further innovation, three pages of dramatic picture stories including 'Pauline's Peril'; unfortunately he drew them all himself. But the gamble paid off: after nine issues *Bouncer* and all the other Target publications (including the give-away *Ovaltiney's Own Comic*) vanished from the newsagents' counters. A.P. had bought them up; from 8th April, 1939, the Bath comics were no more.

22

THE DANDY: OUR FUNSTERS' WILES
WILL BRING YOU SMILES!

Of all the outsiders in the comic publishing game, none could be further outside than D. C. Thomson and Co. Ltd. This family firm is situated in Dundee, Scotland, a long way from Fleetway House, Farringdon Street, home of the Amalgamated Press. Perhaps because of this very fact of geography, Thomson's comics still remain untouched by city sophistication and close to the hearts of British children everywhere.

Thomson's had done very well with a string of boys' story weeklies which they cheerfully called their 'Big Five': *Wizard, Hotspur, Rover, Skipper* and *Adventure*. All papers had comic strips as fillers, usually drawn by the same stylish artist, Allan Morley. He had 'Wishbone Wuzzy' in *Hotspur*, 'Nosey Parker' in *Rover*, and no fewer than three in *Wizard*, which sported a full centre-spread in overlaid red: 'Nero and Zero the Rollicking Romans', 'Softie Simpkins', and 'Happy Harry the Newsreel Cameraman'. Thomson's also included a fold-up, pull-out comic in their *Sunday Post*. This featured two full-page strips, 'Oor Wullie' and 'The Broons', both drawn and written in thick Scots dialect by Dudley D. Watkins.

The first Thomson comic was a give-away, *The Midget Comic*, a 32-page pocket-size booklet presented free with *Rover* on 11th February, 1933. It contained strips by Watkins ('Tell-Tale Timothy') and Morley ('Freddy Fluence the Boy Mesmerist'), and was successful enough to warrant a follow-up on 21st December, 1935, *Nosey Parker's Midget Comic*. Finally, on 4th December, 1937, came number one of *The Dandy*: 28 pages, full colour cover, red overlay centre and back, price twopence. The page size was 8 inches wide by 11¾ inches deep, matching the Thomson 'Big Five'.

There had been a number of ill-fated attempts to produce comics in the half-tabloid format, from the original *Chips* to *Playtime*. A.P. had finally found success with *Film Fun* (17th January, 1920) and its companion *Kinema Comic* (24th April, 1920), but not with their third cinema-based paper *Film Picture Stories* (28th July, 1934), or their athletic imitation, *Sports Fun* (11th February, 1922). These were all black-and-white comics and were considered by the A.P. to be picture papers for the adolescent and adult rather than comics for children. Certainly they mystified me as a child; I had never heard of such strange personalities as 'Wheeler and Woolsey', 'Joe E. Brown', or even 'Laurel and Hardy', and I found the

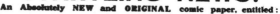

NO. 1 TUESDAY, JANUARY 13th!

All the REAL Film Favourites in Pictures of Funniosity.
"Film Fun" strikes an entirely new note in both humorous
and cinema papers.

🖙 NOTHING ELSE LIKE IT ON THE MARKET 🖘

11. Cinema Comic: advertisement for number one of 'Film Fun', 13th January, 1920; drawn by G. W. Wakefield.

drawing of such artists as G. W. Wakefield over-careful in its striving for a likeness which meant little to me. *The Dandy,* however, was a different kettle of comics.

'Korky the Kat' led off the big parade of pictorial fun in that number one, just as he still does today. Inside there was work by Watkins (his 'Desperate Dan' the cow-pie guy of Cactusville is now legend) and Morley ('Keyhole Kate' was the first in a long line of Thomson psychotics), with picture stories drawn by 'Big Five' story illustrators: 'The Daring Deeds of Buck Wilson' was a vigorous western, while 'Lost on the Mountain of Fear' introduced monster spiders and other horrors the like of which would not be seen in A.P. comics for twenty more years.

The first *Beano* arrived on 30th July, 1938, following the *Dandy* blueprint both as to format and form (Plate 12). The front page animal was 'Big Eggo', an awkward ostrich drawn by Reg Carter, and inside Watkins had the memorable 'Lord Snooty and his Pals'; Morley drew 'Big Fat Joe'. For picture serials there were 'Cracker Jack the Wonder Whip Man', 'Wild Boy of the Woods', and 'Morgyn the Mighty'. This Tarzan type had been a popular hero in stories in *Rover,* as had *Dandy's* 'Jimmy and his Grockle'. This translation of a story hero into picture strips, a favourite trick of Thomson's, reached its ultimate when *Wizard's* long-running 'Wilson' started all over again as a cartoon hero. Finally the 'Big Five' themselves converted from story papers into comics.

12. Dundee's 'Dandy': advertisement for number one, 3rd December, 1937.

Meanwhile the Amalgamated Press was not idle. It fought back in Thomson's own format with *Radio Fun* (15th October, 1938): 28 pages for twopence with a full colour front page animal. 'George the Jolly Gee-Gee' could hardly be called a radio star, but the artwork by Roy Wilson more than made up for this error (Plate 13). Later Reg Parlett shifted his 'Big-Hearted Arthur Askey' from the red-tinted back to the four-colour front and the comic settled down to a run which only died because radio died too (18th February, 1961). Drawn by the old 'penny black' brigade, *Radio Fun* had all the slapstick vigour lacking in the stereotyped strips of *Film Fun*.

The Knock-Out (4th March, 1939) was A.P.'s second venture into the new format. This time editors and artists lacked the restraint imposed by representing real people, and an entirely new-looking comic was born. The style was set by Hugh McNeil, who drew the page one hero 'Deed-a-Day Danny'. McNeil's style was brisk, refreshing and funny, and although rooted in A.P. tradition, he was encouraged to allow his own personal sense of humour to intrude. Although he did not create the famous series 'Our Ernie, Mrs Entwhistle's Little Lad', it was McNeil's private fantasy that lifted this Wigan Pier-based hero out of the rut and into the wider, wilder world. When McNeil went to war, the late A. J. Kelly took over both Ernie and 'Stonehenge Kit the Ancient Brit', further amplifying their hilarious whimsy. *The Knock-Out* followed the Thomson tradition by picturising the adventures of famous fiction heroes from A.P. boys' weeklies. 'Sexton Blake' and 'Billy Bunter' (as drawn by Frank Minnitt) are today better remembered for their strip appearances than for all their longer literary careers. After an ignoble period as a 'horror comic', *Knock-Out* merged with *Valiant* on 16th February, 1963, although its name alone was revived for a new I.P.C. comic on 12th June, 1971.

Thomson's were undaunted by A. P.'s hopefully-named *Knock-Out* and on 22nd July, 1939 struck back with *The Magic*. The front page animal was 'Koko the Pup': E. H. Banger, adrift since the closure of Target Publications, had clearly found a new home. Watkins was here again with 'Peter Piper—Picking People Out of Pickles', as was Morley with 'Dolly Dimple—Not So Simple!' This time Thomson's had lowered their sights to the nursery market and, incidentally, lowered their page count to 24. To make up, back page and centre spread were in full colour instead of the customary red and black. The declaration of war (3rd September, 1939) put paid to *The Magic* and many other comics, including one which A.P. had brought down to this popular new format,

Crackers. Playbox lasted the war in the reduced size and was later restored to full tabloid glory.

A newly-established quartet of comics published by A. Soloway, *Comic Capers, Comic Adventures, All Star* and *All Fun,* also shrank from tabloid to American comic-book format, adding a second colour to their sixteen pages. Each ran a total of 26 issues between 1939 and 1946, and are well remembered for Nat Brand's excellent picture stories, 'Crash Carew', 'Halcon, Lord of the Crater Land', 'Bentley Price, Detective', and 'Dandy McQueen of the Mounties'. Brand had first appeared in *New Triumph,* A.P.'s short-lived attempt at an American-style comic, where he had drawn a four-page weekly serial, 'Derrickson Dene' (1939-40).

FAMOUS FUNNIES: 100 COMICS—10 CENTS!

The American comic, created as a weapon in the great newspaper war between William Randolph Hearst and Joseph Pulitzer, evolved quite differently from its British counterpart. All they have in common is pictures. Strip cartoons printed in four colours began to appear in the magazine sections of Sunday newspapers following Mark Fenderson's 'On the Tramp' in the *New York World* of 2nd January, 1894. Previous to this, the only colour comics to be seen in the States were the single sheets of picture stories printed in France by Pellerin, and translated into English for distribution by the Humoristic Publishing Company of Kansas City. These sixteen-panel stories (Plate 4) were charmingly drawn and coloured, but hardly suitable to the native temperament, which found readier laughter in the pantomimes about hoboes and hard-headed Negroes drawn by A. B. Frost, R. F. Outcault, and F. B. Opper in the weekly magazines.

It was from *Life, Judge* and *Harper's* that the first newspaper comic artists came, and gradually the idea of recurring characters caught on, replacing the 'miscellaneous' strip cartoons. Richard Outcault's 'Yellow Kid' panel turned into a strip in the *New York Journal's* colour section *The American Humorist* (1897), which was also the birthplace of 'The Katzenjammer Kids', created by Rudolph Dirks on 12th December, 1897. Hans and Fritz, those plagues upon Der Captain and Der Mama, later divided amoeba-like into a second strip, 'The Captain and the Kids', after a precedent-setting law suit. Both series are still running in rival newspapers today, although the original artists, Dirks and Harold Knerr, are no longer alive.

The Adventures of Foxy Grandpa was the first American comic book. It was published in 1900 and contained 39 reprinted adventures of the newspaper strip character created by 'Bunny' (Carl Schultze). It was followed in 1904 by *Buster Brown, His Dog Tige, and their Troubles* (Plate 5), some fifteen strips from the *New York Herald,* for which Richard Outcault had first drawn his mischievous pair on 4th May, 1902. There were many succeeding volumes, published in America by Frederick Stokes and distributed in England by William Chambers. The Sunday supplements also came to England and were sold in market places up and down the country at two a penny. Thus many American characters attained great popularity in England without any official distribution or reprinting in the British press. 'Buster Brown' was pirated by *Puck* as 'Scorcher Smith', and Opper's famous tramp 'Happy Hooligan' (1899) turned up in *The Big Budget* as 'Happy Ike'.

As the Sunday funnies section grew in size, so it changed in character: while strips with child-appeal remained, new ones were introduced to bring in the rest of the family. Bud Fisher's 'Mutt and Jeff' was aimed at the betting fraternity, and Cliff Sterrett's 'Polly and her Pals' at the family man with an eye for a pretty miss, while George Herriman's 'Krazy Kat' was strictly for the sophisticates. Meeting favour at every level was Winsor McCay's 'Little Nemo in Slumberland', the first strip to raise the American comic to an art.

The American comic was given away free with your Sunday paper; the British comic was sold at the newsagents like any other magazine. George Delacorte Jr. noted the difference. As the Dell Publishing Company he already had a string of pulp and popular magazines, and on 16th January, 1929 a new title appeared alongside them: *The Funnies*. It was a weekly tabloid of 24 pages, eight of them in full colour, and it sold at 10 cents. On the front page was a 9-panel serial, 'Frosty Ayre', drawn by Joe Archibald, and inside was a mixture of strips, jokes, serials and type-set stories. It was modelled on the British comic, but with an American approach—and it was a flop. Various experiments were tried: the page count went up to 32; the cover strip was dropped in favour of a single cartoon; it went on to a fortnightly schedule, then monthly, then weekly; the price was halved and so was the page-count. But still it flopped, and finally expired on reaching number 36. Copies of the comic they could not give away are today worth a fortune to the ever-increasing breed of comic collectors!

The next American comic-books were indeed given away:

they were compilations of newspaper strips, reduced in size to fit a folded tabloid approximately $7\frac{1}{2}$ inches wide by $10\frac{1}{4}$ inches deep. Produced by M. C. Gaines for such agencies as Procter and Gamble, these 64-page booklets were handed out as 'premiums' by grocery chain-stores. One of the series, given the title of *Famous Funnies,* was overprinted and Gaines stuck labels on them: '10 Cents'. These were snapped up from those news-stands willing enough to take a chance on the little books, and Gaines realised he had found the winning formula for the American comic. Previous experiments had been too close in format to the tabloid section given free with every Sunday newspaper; his half-tabloid booklet looked new and different, even if the material was second-run reprints. In November, 1934 the Eastern Color Printing Co. of 50 Church Street, New York, published *Famous Funnies* No. 1. It ran for 218 issues! The front and back covers, drawn by Jon Mayes, were the only original items in the 68-page magazine. The '100 Comics and Games, Puzzles, Magic' of the subtitle were all syndicated reprints, beginning on page two with 'Toonerville Folks' and ending on page 67 with 'Mutt and Jeff'. Later some original artwork was introduced ('Seaweed Sam the Rhyming Rover' by 'Vep' and 'Fearless Flint' by H. G. Peter) but the comic remained essentially a reprint magazine for all its long life (Plate 14).

Similar compilations of newspaper strips with a smattering of original pages were launched during 1935 by Dell (February: *Popular Comics),* United Features (April: *Tip Top Comics),* David McKay (May: *King Comics),* and Dell again (October: *The Funnies).* 1937 brought Dell's *The Comics* (March), McKay's *Ace Comics* (April), and Comic Favourites' *Feature Funnies* (October), while 1938 saw the first issues of United's *Comics On Parade* (April), Whitman's *Super Comics* (May), and Dell's *Crackajack Funnies* (June).

While these comic-books are all of enormous historic interest in that they collate and preserve in convenient form the large-size newspaper comic pages, of greater intrinsic value are those American comic-books containing original art. The first of these, following the *Funnies* flop, oddly enough followed the *Funnies* format. Malcolm Wheeler-Nicholson, a pulp story author, financed by a Brooklyn newspaper, published his *More Fun Magazine* in February 1935 as a tabloid. Again he followed the British comic paper formula by introducing text stories and features, together with a front page comic strip, 'Little Linda' by Whitney Ellsworth. Inside no picture story ran more than one page, which made his monthly publication schedule a long gap between episodes of the serials. These included 'Sandra of the Secret Service' by C. Brigham, 'Don Drake on the Planet Saro' by Clemens Gretter, and 'Doctor Occult the Ghost Detective' by Leger and Reuths—pseudonyms for Jerome Siegel and Joe Shuster, names to conjure with. The pages, only eighteen of which were in colours, also included a large picture drawn by a young Walt Kelly, in later years the creator of 'Pogo'.

New Comics, Nicholson's second venture, began in December 1935, and was the first fully original comic-book in the smaller *Famous Funnies* format. It had 80 pages and sold for ten cents. *More Fun* sheared a few inches off its length in January 1936, then came down to match *New Comics* in size with the March issue (number 9). The original heroes of *New Comics* included 'Captain Jim of the Texas Rangers' by Homer Fleming, who also drew 'Sandor and the Lost Civilization', and Siegel and Shuster's 'Federal Men'. The accent was on the dramatic picture serial and it changed its name to *New Adventure Comics* from January 1937.

The trend towards the picture story had begun in the third issue of *Funny Pages* (July 1936), which had started two months earlier as *The Comics Magazine.* In this historic issue the standard pattern of the two-page story was suddenly interrupted by a special full-page announcement: 'Frontier Justice —a seven-page complete story of the West in beautifully graphic pictures. This brand new form of cartoon-style complete story telling is original with *The Comics Magazine Funny Pages.'* The publishers then requested readers to write letters discussing 'this new departure in fiction form'. That they did so, and in approving terms, is demonstrated by the publishers' introduction in November 1936 of *Funny Picture Stories,* the first all-original, all-dramatic picture strip comic-book. W. M. Allison, who had drawn 'Frontier Justice', was present with 'Wild Horse', but of greater interest is 'Alias the Clock' by George E. Brenner: the first of many mysterious masked heroes in American comics. 'The Clock' turned up in *Detective Picture Stories* (December 1936), but not in a third companion magazine, *'Western Picture Stories'* (February 1937).

Wow!—subtitled 'What a Magazine!'—a hotch-potch of reprints and originals published from August 1936, is notable for its introduction to comic art of William Eisner. His early strips 'The Flame' and 'Captain Scott Dalton' show something of the shadowy, expressionistic atmosphere he would develop in his later newspaper supplement series 'The Spirit'. Eisner is a key figure in American comic-book history, both as an artist, an art editor, a character creator, and a style-setter. He next appeared with western and detective strips in those Comics

13. *Dramatic Comic: first American comic magazine to feature serious strips: 'Funny Picture Stories' number one, November 1936; cover by George Brenner.*

— BUT WITH THE SPEED OF
A SPRINGING PANTHER,
THE HAWK FLINGS HIMSELF ACROSS
THE ROOM ——

WHY YOU ONE
EYED FREAK-THE
IDEA OF TORTURING
A LITTLE GIRL AND
AN OLD MAN-I'LL
CUT YOU TO
RIBBONS!

14. *Early Heroes: Hawks of the Seas by Will ('Spirit') Eisner; Peter Pupp by Bob ('Batman') Kane; from 'Wags', 1937.*

Magazine Co's publications mentioned in the previous paragraph, then drew the weekly 'Hawks of the Seas' serial for *Wags* (1937), a comic paper produced in America for export only. These tabloid pages were reprinted in *Jumbo Comics* from September 1938, a large format comic which also ran the early 'Peter Pupp' serial by Bob Kane (later creator of 'Batman'), despite the fact that they had already been run, and in colour instead of the original black-and-white, in *Feature Funnies* from November 1937. Eisner's several detective and western series were also reprinted in *Keen Detective Funnies,* one of the Centaur group.

Centaur had taken over the Comics Magazine Co. chain, along with *Star Comics* and *Star Ranger,* two excellent but larger-format comic-books published by Harry A. Chesler. Centaur was run by Joseph Hardie, 'Uncle Joe', and although primarily concerned with reprinting strips which already looked older than their two to three years, he initiated the first all science-fiction comic *Amazing Mystery Funnies* (August 1938). 'Skyrocket Steele' and 'Dirk the Demon' were both drawn by Bill Everett, who would attain greater fame in the age of the super-hero as the creator of 'The Sub-Mariner'. This period, which to some collectors signifies the start of a Golden Age of American Comics, to others the end, began on the cover of *Action Comics* number one, dated June 1938. The writer, Jerome Siegel; the artist, Joe Shuster; the hero, 'Superman'.

1. *World's first comic book: Marie Duval's cover for 'Some Playful Episodes in the Career of Ally Sloper,' a collection of strips from 'Judy', published November 1873.*

2. *Britain's first comic paper: Procter's front page cartoon for 'Funny Folks' number 12, published by James Henderson, 27th February, 1875.*

ALF AND BILLY TRY TO CELEBRATE THE NEW CENTURY BY BEING VERY, VERY GOOD. WHAT HO!

3. *New century comic: first 'Big Budget' of 1901, 5th January; front page by 'Yorick' (Ralph Hodgson).*

Jack Simpleton is a big boy fifteen years old but so stupid that his parents do not know what to do with him.

His mother told him one day to go to the house of the nurse and fetch home his baby brother. "As you are good for nothing else perhaps you may be able to do this."

Jack started off and on the way met the nurse who said: "Go to the house and you will find your brother in the cradle."

While Jack is idling away his time on the road, a monkey enters the room in which the baby is and looks with wonder at the little child.

The child begins to cry. The monkey takes him, undresses him and lays him under the cradle. He then wraps himself in the sheets and takes the baby's place.

At length Jack arrives and looking with amazement into the cradle shouts: "O! my little brother has whiskers already!"

He carries the monkey away swinging him to and fro in his arms to make him sleep; but the monkey, not enjoying this, bites his nose.

Jack becomes angry and wishes to whip him: but the monkey runs up into a tree and ascends to the uppermost branch.

On his knees Jack begs him to come down but the monkey will not and only makes wry faces at him.

Jack now takes a stone and throws it with such force at the monkey that he falls lifeless to the ground.

Filled with grief and despair at the result of his rash act, he carries the body to the best doctor in the neighbourhood.

The physician thinking that he is being made a fool of, orders his servant to put him out.

Jack runs off and arriving at his home is met by his parents who ask "Where is your brother?"

I have killed him. He was too bad to live. Jack answered and threw the monkey to the floor.

His mother faints away while his father seizes a big hickory stick and prepares to chastise his inhuman son.

At this moment the nurse enters with the true baby and the innocence and simplicity of poor Jack are established.

"Printed expressly for the Humoristic Publishing Co, Kansas City, Mo."

4. *First American comic: 'Jack Simpleton', number 34 of a series of coloured sheets, printed in France for American distribution (date unknown).*

5. *Early American comic: a coloured Sunday section from
'The New York Herald' newspaper, 26th June, 1904;
'Buster Brown' by R. F. Outcault.*

1ᴰ PUCK

No. 83. Vol. IV.   EVERY FRIDAY. ONE PENNY.   FEBRUARY 24th, 1906.

GRANDPA JONES IS LET INTO A FEW SECRETS BY THE CASEYITES.

6. *First successful British coloured comic: 'Puck' number 83, 24th February, 1906, starring Johnny Jones and the Casey Court Kids, by H. O'Neill.*

7. *'The Rainbow': ninth issue of the famous coloured comic featuring the Bruin Boys by Julius Stafford Baker, 11th April, 1914.*

8. *Special edition: Mickey's eighth birthday as a film mouse celebrated in number 34 of 'Mickey Mouse Weekly', 26th September, 1936, the first British gravure comic; cover painted by Wilfred Haughton.*

9. 'Happy Days': first Christmas issue of the Amalgamated Press's first full colour gravure comic; drawn by Roy Wilson, 31st December, 1938.

10. *British newspaper comic: Coronation issue of the 'Teddy Tail' comic given free with the 'Daily Mail', 1st May, 1937. Drawn by H. S. Foxwell.*

11. 2500th celebration issue of 'Comic Cuts', 16th April, 1938; drawn by 'Charlie' Pease.

12. Dundee 'Beano': early issue of the famous D. C. Thomson comic, the only title in this pictorial section which is still running; cover by Reg Carter, 15th October, 1938.

13. First issue of the first radio comic: 'Radio Fun', 15th October, 1938; drawn by Roy Wilson. A.P.'s half-tabloid answer to Thomson's 'Beano', published the same week as the comic opposite.

14. *First American comics magazine: number one of 'Famous Funnies', November 1934; drawn by Jon Mayes.*

15. *First British American-style comic magazine: number one of 'New Funnies', February 1904; drawn by Wood.*

16. First horror comic: the first issue of 'Vault of Horror',
April 1950, numbering continued from its previous titling,
'War Against Crime'; cover by Johnny Craig.

ACTION COMICS: IT'S A BIRD! IT'S A PLANE! IT'S SUPERMAN!

The story of Superman's origin is a double one. How Siegel and Shuster peddled their concept around from editor to editor for five years before M. C. Gaines passed their sketches over to Harry Donenfeld, then assembling a companion comic-book for his *Detective Comics* (No. 1 March 1937). How a scientist on the planet Krypton placed his infant son in a rocket ship, shooting him to Earth just as that planet exploded. Raised by the kindly Kents, the boy called Clark used his extra-terrestrial powers to combat crime in the costume of Superman. His success was instant, as was his creators'. His tale was told again in his own comic-book, *Superman* (November 1938), in a daily newspaper strip, a Sunday colour page, an English comic reprint in *New Triumph,* a radio serial, a novel, a Big Little Book, a cartoon film, a live-action serial, a television series, and countless revamped versions in succeeding special editions of *Action* and other comics. His like was instantly revamped for so many rival comic-book heroes that their names alone would be sufficient to fill the rest of this book.

His greatest rival was spawned within his own publisher's empire. 'Batman' was created by Bob Kane for *Detective Comics* No. 27 (May 1939); by Spring 1940 he had his own book: *Batman* No. 1. A female counterpart was created for the first issue of *Sensation Comics* (January 1942) and soon 'Wonder Woman' too had her own quarterly comic (Summer 1942). Outside rivals included 'Captain America', created by Jack Kirby and Joe Simon for *Captain America Comics* (March 1941), and the most famous of them all, 'Captain Marvel', who first appeared at newsboy Billy Batson's cry of 'Shazam!' in the pages of *Whiz Comics* for February 1940. This magical hero spawned a family of super-people. There was 'Captain Marvel Jr.' (born *Whiz Comics* December 1941), 'Mary Marvel' (born *Captain Marvel* 18th December, 1942), 'Uncle Marvel' and even 'Hoppy the Marvel Bunny'. But perhaps his most unlikely offspring was his British cousin, 'Marvelman'.

The American comic-book was sold in England at twopence a time up to the outbreak of war in September 1939. Instantly imports ceased. The impact of the American comic upon English readers had been great, but upon English publishers small. The first British comic to utilise the pocketable trans-

49

15. Superman Is Born: cover of 'Action Comics' number one, June 1938; by Joe Shuster.

atlantic format was *Flash Comics,* a shoddily printed and poorly drawn affair published during 1939 by the Camden Magazine Co. In January 1940 came the first issue of *New Funnies* (Plate 15) by Gerald G. Swan. This 64-page job, printed in black but bound in a coloured cover, sold at six-pence and was quite a success in a comic-starved country. It led Swan to a string of titles, all of which began as monthlies, but as paper controls tightened, turned into undated, 32-page quarterlies selling at 3d. *Topical Funnies* came second followed by *War Comics, Thrill Comics, Slick Fun, Fresh Fun,* and *Extra Fun.* They all followed the American formula (excluding four-colour interiors) and shared a pool of cartoon-ists and characters. These included William Ward, an ex-animator for 'Bonzo' films, who drew both funnies ('Sheriff Fox') and picture serials ('Iron Man'), Murdock Stimpson who did the same with less success ('Tough Guys' and 'Flash Scar-

50

16. *British Comic-book: first issue of 'Topical Funnies', April 1940; cover by John Woods.*

lett'), and E. H. Banger, who had been the 'Roy Wilson' of the pre-war Target Publications. Like the others, Banger was expected to mix comedy ('Coal Black Jones') and drama ('Slicksure'), but unlike the others he did it in the same strips!

After the war a rash of new publishers appeared on the English comic scene. Some, like Martin and Reid, aped the old-style Amalgamated Press comics with *Jolly Chuckles* (1946) and *Super Star* (1948); others, like Cartoon Art Productions, followed the hero trend with *Super-Duper* (1947), which ran Dennis M. Reader's 'Powerman'. L. Miller and Son had been reprinting Fawcett publications in handsome two-tone photogravure: *Whiz, Wow,* and, of course, *Captain Marvel*. Suddenly there came news of final victory in a long-running law suit: Superman had ultimately overpowered Captain Marvel. Even the magic word 'Shazam' could not save Billy Batson now. His publishers, Fawcett, had capitulated out of court and surrendered to the man of steel. L. Miller and Son, acting with all speed, called in the services of an ex-commando art agent and tyro cartoonist, Maurice 'Mick' Anglo. The next week's edition of Miller's weekly *Captain Marvel* comic bore two overprinted words: 'The' and 'Man'. Two weeks later, on 6th February, 1954, it was called *Marvelman*—and a brand new, all-British super-hero was born. Where Billy Batson had cried 'Shazam' and turned into Captain Marvel, now Micky Moran cried 'Kimota' and turned into Marvelman! A legend began, one which lasted for 300 issues or more; one which makes *Marvelman* (1954), crude as it was, one of the best-remembered and most collected of all British comics.

17. *American Superhero: Billy Batson cries "Shazam!", and Captain Marvel is born; drawn by C. C. Beck.*

18. *British Super-
hero: Micky
Moran cries
"Kimota!" and
Marvelman is
born; drawn by
R. Parker.*

Mick Anglo was at the creative centre of many independent British comics modelled on the American school, from
Paget Publications' *Wonderman* (1948) and the Arnold Book
Company's *Space Comics* (1953) to his own publication
Captain Miracle (1960). The hundreds of comic-books he
turned out are given a curious similarity by his insistence on
inking all the lettering himself, no matter if the artist be
excellent (Don Lawrence) or otherwise (myself). This editorial
idiosyncracy was due more to economics than egoism;
fortunately it was not allowed to mar Anglo's best production,
TV Tornado (1967), which was financed by City Magazines.

A more stylish art agency was King-Ganteaume ,who pro-
vided a comic-book service for Miller *(Bulldog Brittain)* and
Scion *(Electroman)*. The latter publisher issued the early work
of such later strip stylists as Ron Embleton and James
Holdaway. Classiest of the many independents who rose during
and after the war was Philip Marx, under whose imprints of
Philmar, P. M. Productions, and Amex, appeared well-printed
comics by many A.P. cartoonists who were finding a full
week's work hard to come by under the size-reduced, paper-
controlled conditions that then prevailed. Marx's editor was
a former A.P. man, John Garbutt, and he kept his comics
up to the high standards of his old firm. However, *Flash* (1948)
was his only title to achieve anything like a good run: it
folded after 11 issues despite doubling its page size to tabloid
and bursting into full colour gravure.

EAGLE: THE NEW NATIONAL STRIP CARTOON WEEKLY !

The first real post-war threat to the comic monopolies of the Amalgamated Press and D. C. Thomson came, as had the Target comics, from the provinces. J. B. Allen, using a quirk in the law to obtain a precious paper quota, converted a defunct newspaper into *The Comet,* launching it as a fortnightly comic from 20th September, 1946 from 10, Queen's Road, Sale, Cheshire. It was an eight page sub-tabloid (9¼″ by 12″), front and back overlaid with red. The first cover was 'The Old Timer' drawn by Alan Fraser, an individual but amateurish artist first seen in the comic section of the *South Wales Echo* during 1935. A pictorial adaptation of Stevenson's 'Treasure Island' which ran on page eight was drawn by Bob Wilkin, who had grown familiar through many minor comic-books drawn during the war (including the hopefully-prophetic *Victory Funnies*). Allen's publication was a great success and went into two-tone gravure from number 15; this improved the look of Beaumont's front page serial, 'Jungle Lord'. Allen now went into weekly production by starting a new comic to appear on alternate weeks. To do this he converted another pre-war publication, a health magazine called *Fitness and Sun.* The new *Sun* shone in gravure from the start, 11th November, 1947, and Wilkin took page one with his adaptation of 'The Swiss Family Robinson'. Inside, an old friend, Banger, showed up with 'Old Buck and Texas Tich, Our Prairie Pals'. The two comics continued to improve until eventually they were bought up by A.P. with effect from 22nd May, 1949.

Comet and *Sun* were absorbed into the *Knock-Out* editorial department, which soon showed its influence by introducing old characters like Eric R. Parker's 'Patsy and Tim' and reprints of Kelly's 'Pin-Up Jokes'. But better things were on the way: 'Buck Jones' and 'June', (drawn by Norman Pett of the *Daily Mirror's* 'Jane'), both began in the August 13th issue of *Comet,* as did A.P.'s first American-style super-hero, 'Thunderbolt Jaxon', an unusual departure for funny-man Hugh McNeil. McNeil also drew 'Deadshot Sue' for *Sun,* but was really more at home with 'Young Joey—Always Late for School', a reworking of his 'Our Ernie'. This revamped series was revamped yet again as 'Slowcoach' in *Whizzer and Chips,* drawn by Peter Maddocks. *Sun* and *Comet* went through many remodellings, including a long run in the smaller American comic-book format, before winding up together on 17th October, 1959.

Meanwhile in America the super-hero was dying of the one disease to which he was vulnerable: failing circulation. A new boom had begun with so-called 'True Crime Comics', and out of these had emerged an even more unsettling type of comic-book, the 'Horror Comic'. William Gaines, son of the pioneering *Famous Funnies* man, had taken over his father's firm, Educational Comics. He kept the initials E.C. but switched Educational for Entertaining, abandoning such series as *Picture Stories from the Bible* in favour of *The Vault of Horror* (Plate 16). Those concerned with child welfare, psychology and education, championed by Dr. Fredric Wertham in America and Rev. Marcus Morris in England, agitated vigorously in press and public. Ultimately the 'Horror Comics Bill' was pushed through Parliament and the importation of all American comics into Great Britain was stopped. In America the Comics Code Authority was established to clean up the comic-books by use of its seal of approval; in England Marcus Morris established *Eagle*.

'Dan Dare, Pilot of the Future' rocketed off the full colour photogravure front page of *Eagle* number one on 14th April, 1950. The clean linework of Frank Hampson established a new standard of comic art in England, and Frank Bellamy and many other modern masters sprang from this school. 'The New National Strip Cartoon Weekly', as it was headlined, was a return to full tabloid size, and ran to 20 pages, eight of them in four colours, for threepence. Edward Hulton, proprietor of *Picture Post,* published and Marcus Morris edited, introducing a Biblical strip on the back page, 'The Great Adventurer'. *Eagle* brought a pre-war touch of class to the post-war British comic, and soon spawned spin-offs to embrace every type of reader: *Girl* (2nd November, 1951), *Robin* (28th March, 1953), and *Swift* (20th March, 1954). All were clean and elegant to look at, being both drawn and printed with care.

Morris and Hulton's idea of publishing comics aimed at specific age and sex groups interested the Amalgamated Press, who changed their fiction magazine *School Friend* into the first comic specifically for the schoolgirl (20th May, 1950). They followed it with another strip-job on *Girl's Crystal* (21st March, 1953) but this one failed after only eight weeks. *Lion* (23rd February, 1952) was their first picture story paper for boys, and it ultimately devoured *Eagle,* in whose space-age image it had been created. *News of the World* was a surprising entrant into the comic market, launching television's first post-war hero 'Muffin the Mule' as cover star of its gravure *TV Comic* (9th November, 1951). A.P. answered this new

19. *'Eagle' Arrives: advertisement for number one in parent magazine 'Picture Post', 15th April, 1950.*

challenger with *TV Fun*, modelled, of course, on *Radio Fun*. Commencing 19th September, 1953 it switched in 1960 to *TV Fan*, a romance comic for teenage girls.

Thomson's first post-war comic came on 2nd February, 1953: *Topper* was also their first venture into tabloid size. Although this had been the predominating page size pre-war, it came fresh again in the fifties now that A.P. had entirely gone over to *Dandy* proportions. *Topper* was joined by *Beezer* on 21st January, 1956. A.P.'s first new comic for the nursery market was *Jack and Jill* (27th February, 1954), joined by *Playhour Pictures* later the same year (16th October). These colour gravure comics succeeded where, long before, the pioneering *Happy Days* had failed. *Tiger* (11th September, 1954) was an obvious companion for *Lion*, and the first

56

romantic picture story paper for teenage girls was *Marilyn* (19th March, 1955). Another newspaper came into comics with *Junior Express* (18th June, 1955), which later reflected showbiz trends by becoming *TV Express* (23rd April, 1960). By then it had incorporated another *Eagle* imitator, *Rocket* (21st April, 1956). That very first gravure comic, *Mickey Mouse,* now sub-divided after a court case. Odhams retained their non-Disney characters and re-launched them in *Zip* (4th January, 1958), while another publisher took on *Walt Disney's Mickey Mouse* from the same date. *Bunty* (18th January, 1958) was Thomson's comic for the younger schoolgirl and *Top Spot* (25th October, 1958) was A.P.'s comic for the younger man. *Bunty* is still with us; *Top Spot* is not. In England the maturing male seems not yet ready for a comic; comics remain fixed as juvenilia, although the pocket-size 'library' comic-book has become increasingly popular with teenagers since *Cowboy Comics* began with 'Buck Jones' in April 1950. Thomson's introduced their first all-pictorial paper for boys on 24th October, 1959: *New Hotspur*, a revamping of the 'old'. The first nursery comic to reflect the influence of the animated cartoon film was *Harold Hare's Own Paper* (14th November, 1959), although Hugh McNeil had created his funny bunny for an earlier and more mature comic.

POW! FOR THE NEW BREED OF COMIC FANS!

In the decade beginning January 1960 no fewer than 63 new weekly comics have been launched in Britain. Too many to discuss in detail, a chronological list of the titles is appended, together with publisher and first issue date information, at the end of this chapter. But as the fifties belonged to *Eagle* and Frank Hampson, so the sixties belong to *Wham* and Leo Baxendale. This prolific cartoonist began in *Beano* with 'The Three Bears', a wacky and wild affair owing as much to the weird world of Warner Brothers cartoons as to the style of Giles of the *Daily Express*. Baxendale soon modelled *Dandy* and *Beano* after his own image: the spotty, blotty kid, eternally at war with parent-teacher authority. When Odhams re-entered the comic field with *Wham* (20th June, 1964), it was Baxendale who drew practically the entire 24 pages. They followed through with *Smash* (5th February, 1966) and then *Pow* (21st January, 1967), though this one had the very British Baxendale playing second fiddle to the very American *Spiderman*.

In America Stan Lee, editor of Martin Goodman's 'Marvel'

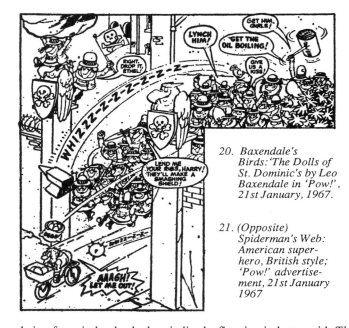

20. Baxendale's
    Birds:'The Dolls of
    St. Dominic's by Leo
    Baxendale in 'Pow!',
    21st January, 1967.

21. (Opposite)
    Spiderman's Web:
    American super-
    hero, British style;
    'Pow!' advertise-
    ment, 21st January
    1967

chain of comic-books, had revitalised a flagging industry with *The Fantastic Four* (November 1961). This rather poorly-drawn comic somehow struck a nerve and sparked off a whole new 'Marvel Age of Comicdom'. All the old super-heroes of the forties were trotted out of retirement and given a new sixties slant, from *Captain America* on down. Although Miller was distributing the American originals in England, Odhams decided to reprint them. They added *Fantastic* (18th February, 1967) and *Terrific* (15th April, 1957) to their roster, carrying 'Thor', 'Iron Man', and 'X-Men' in the one, 'Sub-Mariner', 'Doctor Strange', and 'The Avengers' in the other. 'The new breed of comic fans' as editors 'Alf and Cos' liked to call their readers, suffered a blow when the *Daily Mirror* took over both Odhams and Fleetway (formerly the A.P.). Comics folded, combined, amalgamated; even *Eagle* vanished into its old competitor, *Lion*.

The first new comic to carry the I.P.C. imprint was *Bobo Bunny* (22nd March, 1969). This, the first nursery title to be printed in full colour gravure throughout, heralded the way many future comics would be constructed. It was an international co-production originating in Holland. As costs of paper and printing increased, so the modern comic became more international in flavour. Spanish cartoonists drew for the very British *Cor* (6th June, 1970), while Arthur Martin's 'Bessie Bunter' turns up as 'Fina' in the Spanish comic *Lily* (1971). The English comic *Laurel and Hardy* was a continuation under license of an American original, scripted in London, drawn in Barcelona, printed in Poland, and issued in Italy as *Stanlio e Ollio!*

59

Judy	Thomson	16th January, 1960
Marty	City	23rd January, 1960
Princess	Fleetway	30th January, 1960
Buster	Fleetway	28th May, 1960
TV Land	TV	1st October, 1960
Cherie	Thomson	1st October, 1960
Rover & Adventure	Thomson	21st January, 1961
Victor	Thomson	25th February, 1961
Bimbo	Thomson	18th March, 1961
June	Fleetway	18th March, 1961
Wonderland	Holding	15th September, 1961
Huckleberry Hound	City	7th October, 1961
Serenade	Fleetway	22nd September, 1962
Valiant	Fleetway	6th October, 1962
Yogi Bear's Own	City	27th October, 1962
Treasure	Fleetway	19th January, 1963
Boys' World	Odhams	26th January, 1963
Diana	Thomson	23rd February, 1963
Hornet	Thomson	14th September, 1963
Teddy Bear	Fleetway	21st September, 1963
Poppet	Fleetway	5th October, 1963
Jackie	Thomson	11th January, 1964
Hurricane	Fleetway	29th February, 1964
Wham	Odhams	20th June, 1964
The Big One	Fleetway	17th October, 1964
Sparky	Thomson	23rd January, 1965
TV Century 21	City	23rd January, 1965
Ranger	Fleetway	18th September, 1965
Story Time	Odhams	11th September, 1965
Lady Penelope	City	22nd January, 1966
Smash	Odhams	5th February, 1966
Champion	Fleetway	26th February, 1966
TV Toyland	Fleetway	28th May, 1966
Pippin	Polystyle	29th September, 1966
TV Tornado	City	14th January, 1967
Candy	City	21st January, 1967
Pow	Odhams	21st January, 1967
Mandy	Thomson	21st January, 1967
Fantastic	Odhams	18th February, 1967
Solo	City	18th February, 1967
Tina	Fleetway	25th February, 1967

Terrific	Odhams	15th April, 1967
Giggle	Fleetway	29th April, 1967
Princess Tina	Fleetway	23rd September, 1967
Playland	Polystyle	13th January, 1968
Twinkle	Thomson	27th January, 1968
Jag	Fleetway	27th April, 1968
Joe 90	City	18th January, 1969
Bobo Bunny	IPC	22nd March, 1969
Sally	IPC	14th June, 1969
Whizzer & Chips	IPC	18th October, 1969
Scorcher	IPC	10th January, 1970
Wizard	Thomson	14th February, 1970
Cor	IPC	6th June, 1970
Score 'n' Roar	IPC	19th September, 1970
Thunder	IPC	17th October, 1970
Tammy	IPC	6th February, 1971
Countdown	Polystyle	20th February, 1971
Seven	Gresham	20th February, 1971

22. *Enter a Hero: Trailer for the first appearance of Steadfast McStaunch, 'Knock-Out', 2nd September, 1950; drawn by Denis Gifford. Twenty years later Steadfast stomped again — in Scatty Scrapbook in 'Whizzer and Chips'.*

Disneyland	IPC	27th February, 1971
Jet	IPC	1st May, 1971
Esmeralda	Gresham	12th June, 1971
Knockout	IPC	12th June, 1971
Golden Hours	Shelbourne	January, 1972
Little Star	Thomson	29th January, 1972
Sandie	IPC	12th February, 1972
Donald and Mickey	IPC	4th March, 1972
Hey Diddle Diddle	IPC	25th March, 1972
TV Action	Polystyle	1st April 1972
Pixie	IPC	24th June 1972
Mighty World of Marvel	Marvel	7th October, 1972
Toytown	Williams	7th October, 1972
Fun Time	Williams	3rd November, 1972
Lamb Chop	Shelbourne	November, 1972
Debbie	Thomson	17th February, 1973
Spiderman	Marvel	17th February, 1973
Tarkan	Simavi	3rd March, 1973
Shiver and Shake	IPC	10th March, 1973
Pink	IPC	24th March, 1973
Avengers	Marvel	22nd September, 1973
Tom and Jerry	Spotlight	13th October, 1973
Goofy	IPC	20th October, 1973
Noddy	Hudvale	9th March, 1974
Whoopee!	IPC	9th March, 1974
Bonnie	IPC	16th March, 1974
Jinty	IPC	11th May, 1974
Warlord	Thomson	28th September, 1974
Dracula Lives	Marvel	26th October, 1974
Planet of the Apes	Marvel	26th October, 1974
Cracker	Thomson	18th January, 1975
Mates	IPC	5th February, 1975
Vulcan	IPC	1st March, 1975
Battle	IPC	8th March, 1975
Savage Sword of Conan	Marvel	8th March, 1975
Super Heroes	Marvel	8th March, 1975
Noddy Time	Womans Way	16th May, 1975
Monster Fun	IPC	14th June, 1975
Lindy	IPC	21st June, 1975
Kick-Off	Soccer File	16th August, 1975
Donald Duck	IPC	27th September, 1975
Mickey Mouse	IPC	25th October, 1975
Titans	Marvel	25th October, 1975
Toby	IPC	30th January, 1976

Magic	Thomson	31st January, 1976
Action	IPC	14th February, 1976
Bullet	Thomson	14th February, 1976
Spellbound	Thomson	25th September, 1976
Roy of the Rovers	IPC	25th September, 1976
See-Saw	IPC	9th October, 1976
Captain Britain	Marvel	13th October, 1976
Krazy	IPC	16th October, 1976
Oh Boy!	IPC	23rd October, 1976
Blue Jeans	Thomson	22nd January, 1977
Disney Time	IPC	29th January, 1977
2000 A.D.	IPC	26th February, 1977
Fury	Marvel	16th March, 1977
Tarzan	Byblos	11th June, 1977
Plug	Thomson	24th September, 1977
Fantastic Four	Marvel	28th September, 1977
Cheeky	IPC	22nd October, 1977
Scoop	Thomson	21st January, 1978
Misty	IPC	4th February, 1978
Star Wars	Marvel	8th February, 1978
Emma	Thomson	25th February, 1978
My Guy	IPC	4th March, 1978
Target	Polystyle	14th April, 1978
Star Lord	IPC	13th May, 1978
Wheels	Byblos	June, 1978
Rampage	Marvel	7th June, 1978
True War	IPC	17th June, 1978
Fun To Do	IPC	14th October, 1978
The Crunch	Thomson	20th January, 1979
Marvel Comic	Marvel	24th January, 1979
Laurel & Hardy	Byblos	1st March, 1979
Hulk Comic	Marvel	7th March, 1979
Patches	Thomson	10th March, 1979
Tornado	IPC	24th March, 1979
Photo-Love	IPC	31st March, 1979
Penny	IPC	28th April, 1979
Jackpot	IPC	5th May, 1979
Top Soccer	IPC	15th September, 1979
Fun To Know	IPC	15th September, 1979
Tracy	Thomson	6th October, 1979
Lucky Charm	Thomson	16th October, 1979
Red Dagger	Thomson	16th October, 1979
Dr Who	Marvel	17th October, 1979
Viz Comic	Viz	December, 1979

The sixties can be characterised as the 'television age' of British comics, a flowering that followed on from the funnies of the fifties with the blast-off of Gerry Anderson and his science-fiction puppets into what he labelled the 21st century. Linking with City Magazines, a newish company hitherto reprinting such Yankee television favourites as *Huckleberry Hound* (7th October, 1961), Anderson's outfit issued a series of colourful comics starting with *TV Century 21*, number 1 of which was actually dated 23rd January, 2065! Girls were catered for by *Lady Penelope* (22nd January, 1966), youngsters by *Joe 90* (18th January, 1969) and so on. With *Thunderbirds Specials* as well, these comics have become highly collectable in the nineties.

The Seventies were the 'Marvel Age' of British comics, belatedly echoing the success of Stan Lee in the States. From number one of *The Mighty World of Marvel* (7th October, 1972) and its inevitable partner in super-stuff, *Spider-Man Comics Weekly,* which followed a year later (17th February, 1973), the English arm of the American parent has produced dozens of variations on the super-hero theme. Some of them were short-lived, others a long-running success, notably *Star Wars* (8th February, 1978) and its sequel *Return of the Jedi* (22nd June, 1983), sky-riding on the backs of successful sci-fi films.

BRITISH COMICS SINCE 1980

Nutty	Thomson	10th February, 1980
Speed	IPC	23rd February, 1980
Dickory Dock	IPC	1st March, 1980
Photo Secret Love	IPC	15th March, 1980
Forces in Combat	Marvel	15th May, 1980
Sboncyn	(Welsh language)	May, 1980
Marvel Team-up	Marvel	11th September, 1980
Savage Action	Marvel	9th October, 1980
Super Heroes	Egmont	10th October, 1980
Future Tense	Marvel	5th November, 1980
Valour	Marvel	5th November, 1980
Mickey Magazine	IPC	6th December, 1980
Marvel Super Adventure	Marvel	December, 1980
Buddy	Thomson	14th February, 1981
Girl	IPC	14th February, 1981
Captain America	Marvel	25th February, 1981
All War	Byblos	26th February, 1981
Marvel Action	Marvel	1st April, 1981

Marvel Superadventure	Marvel	29th April, 1981
Blockbuster	Marvel	7th May, 1981
Marvel Madhouse	Marvel	21st May, 1981
Teddy Bear's Playtime	IPC	20th June, 1981
Dreamer	IPC	19th September, 1981
Blakes Seven	Marvel	24th September, 1981
Worzel Gummidge	Marvel	1st October, 1981
Heartbeat	IPC	3rd October, 1981
Buttons	Polystyle	3rd October, 1981
Tops	Thomson	10th October, 1981
Ten Four Action	C.B.	11th November, 1981
Pssst!	Never	4th December, 1981
Scooby Doo	Marvel	25th February, 1982
Monster Monthly	Marvel	4th March, 1982
Warrior	Quality	5th March, 1982
Eagle	IPC	27th March, 1982
Incredible Hulk	Marvel	31st March, 1982
Playbox	IPC	3rd April, 1982
Kim	Marvel	24th April, 1982
Wow	IPC	5th June, 1982
Suzy	Thomson	11th September, 1982
Fantastic Four	Marvel	6th October, 1982
Rupert	Marvel	20th October, 1982
Cartoons (supplement)	Mail on Sunday	24th October, 1982
Daredevils	Marvel	2nd December, 1982
Spike	Thomson	22nd January, 1983
Chips Comic	IPC	12th March, 1983
Mighty Thor	Marvel	20th April, 1983
Original X-Men	Marvel	27th April, 1983
Mighty World of Marvel	Marvel	5th May, 1983
Return of the Jedi	Marvel	22nd June, 1983
Load Runner	LR	23rd June, 1983
Top Cat's Comic Show	Marvel	15th September, 1983
Princess	IPC	24th September, 1983
School Fun	IPC	15th October, 1983
Champ	Thomson	24th February, 1984
Playgroup	IPC	24th March, 1984
Scream	IPC	24th March, 1984
Story Land	Marvel	28th March, 1984
Big Ben	Marvel	28th March, 1984
Indiana Jones	Marvel	6th September, 1984
Transformers	Marvel	20th September, 1984
Captain Britain	Marvel	29th November, 1984
Robin	IPC	19th January, 1985

Pepper Street	Thomson	19th January, 1985
Beeb	Polystyle	29th January, 1985
Nikki	Thomson	23rd February, 1985
Getalong Gang	Marvel	20th April, 1985
Marvel Secret Wars	Marvel	27th April, 1985
Super Powers	Marvel	9th August, 1985
My Little Pony	London	5th September, 1985
Enid Blyton's Adventure	London	12th September, 1985
Care Bears	Marvel	7th October, 1985
Hoot	Thomson	26th October, 1985
Barbie	IPC	1st November, 1985
Diceman	IPC	25th January, 1986
Secret Origins	Marvel	7th March, 1986
Spiderman & Droids	Marvel	10th March, 1986
Masters of the Universe	London	27th March, 1986
Sindy	Marvel	19th April, 1986
Oink!	IPC	3rd May, 1986
Funtime	IPC	14th May, 1986
Ace	Modelbrisk	24th July, 1986
2000 A.D. Presents	IPC	18th August, 1986
She-Ra	London	4th September, 1986
Postman Pat	Polystyle	20th September, 1986
Acorn Green	Marvel	11th October, 1986
Mask	IPC	25th October, 1986
Muppet Babies	Marvel	27th October, 1986
Jem	London	30th October, 1986
Thunder Action	Savoy	30th October, 1986
Katy	IPC	31st October, 1986
Sunny	IPC	1st November, 1986
Nipper	IPC	31st January, 1987
My Little Pony & Friends	London	February, 1987
Action Force	Marvel	7th March, 1987
Popples	Marvel	14th March, 1987
Thundercats	Marvel	21st March, 1987
TV Help	Eagerslant	7th May, 1987
Centurions	London	21st May, 1987
Inspector Gadget	Marvel	10th September, 1987
Shoe People	London	17th September, 1987
Madballs	Marvel	17th September, 1987
Donald Duck	London	17th September, 1987
Keypers	Fleetway	September, 1987
Maple Town	Fleetway	17th October, 1987
Thomas the Tank Engine	Marvel	19th October, 1987
Ewoks	Marvel	19th October, 1987

Supernaturals	Fleetway	31st October, 1987
Winnie the Pooh	London	21st February, 1988
Hi!	Thomson	4th March, 1988
Rainbow	London	17th March, 1988
T.V. Fun	London	23rd March, 1988
Visionaries	Marvel	24th March, 1988
Real Ghost Busters	Marvel	26th March, 1988
Alf	Marvel	14th April, 1988
Lady Lovelylocks	Marvel	16th April, 1988
Flintstones	Marvel	7th May, 1988
Galaxy Rangers	Marvel	7th May, 1988
Girl	Fleetway	7th May, 1988
Dragon's Teeth	Marvel	26th May, 1988
Big Comic	Fleetway	11th June, 1988
Superman	London	16th June, 1988
Marvel Bumper Comic	Marvel	21st July, 1988
Batman	London	21st July, 1988
Hotshot	Fleetway	13th August, 1988
Crisis	Fleetway	17th September, 1988
Smooshees	Fleetway	17th September, 1988
Deadline	Fleetway	29th September, 1988
Wildcat	Fleetway	22nd October, 1988
Sylvanian Families	Marvel	22nd October, 1988
Scouse Mouse	Fleetway	22nd October, 1988
Death's Head	Marvel	10th November, 1988
Brain Damage	Galaxy	6th January, 1989
Tick Tock	Thomson	27th January, 1989
Popeye the Sailor	Marvel	February, 1989
Garfield	Ravette	25th March, 1989
Funny Fortnightly	Fleetway	25th March, 1989
Beep! Beep!	Marvel	25th March, 1989
Cartoon Time	Marvel	15th April, 1989
Point Blank	Brown	April, 1989
Smut	Arf	13th May, 1989
It's Wicked	Marvel	20th May, 1989
Mickey Mouse & Friends	London	6th July, 1989
Merry Go Round	London	6th July, 1989
Count Duckula	Celebrity	12th July, 1989
Punisher	Marvel	31st July, 1989
Sleeze Brothers	Epic	July, 1989
Ovide	Celebrity	7th September, 1989
Funday Times (supplement)	Sunday Times	10th September, 1989
Fast Forward	BBC	13th September, 1989
Ring Raiders	Fleetway	16th September, 1989

Bea	Marvel	21st September, 1989
Slimer	Marvel	21st September, 1989
Wisdom of the Gnomes	Celebrity	28th September,1989
Gas	Tristar	29th September, 1989
Rupert	Celebrity	17th October, 1989
Sooty	Celebrity	19th October, 1989
Bog Paper	Marvel	4th November, 1989
Comic Strip	Galaxy	10th November, 1989
Fireman Sam	Marvel	11th November, 1989
Bogie Man	Fatman	16th November, 1989
Dennis	Marvel	30th November, 1989
D.C. Action	London	11th January, 1990
Strip	Marvel	15th January, 1990
Teenage Mutant Turtles	Fleetway	27th January, 1990
World of Wym	Celebrity	22nd February, 1990
Superted	Marvel	10th March, 1990
Popular Fairy Tales	Clearmark	15th March, 1990
Cookie	Clearmark	21st March, 1990
Snoopy	Ravette	29th March, 1990
Tom & Jerry	Clearmark	19th April, 1990
Disney Weekly	London	17th May, 1990
Zones	London	26th May, 1990
Knights of Pendragon	Marvel	14th June, 1990
Revolver	Fleetway	23rd June, 1990
Teddy Club	Ulkutay	28th June, 1990
Willy Fog	Marvel	4th July, 1990
Playdays	BBC	25th July, 1990
Blag	Blag	25th July, 1990

The eighties proved to be a time of flux for the comic industry. Companies came and went, ambitious plans in ashes. Even the major companies had great problems, notably the Scottish company of D. C. Thomson, whose sumptuous photogravure comic *Tops* (10th October 1981; later *TV Tops*), which should have been a major switch-on, proved a costly turn-off. Virtually all their new titles bit the dust, whatever market they were aimed at: *Buddy* (14th February, 1981) for boys, *Nikki* (23rd February, 1985) for girls, *Pepper Street* (19th January, 1985) for the nursery nippers. A worse fate awaited the International Publishing Corporation, heirs to Harmsworth's mighty Amalgamated Press. After a string of flops: *Dickory Dock* (1st March, 1980), *Dreamer* (19th September, 1981), *Scream* (24th March, 1984), and half-hearted revivals of former glories - new series of *Eagle* (27th March, 1982), *Girl* (14th

February, 1981), *Robin* (19th January, 1985) - the company was bought by tycoon Robert Maxwell. Changing the name back to Fleetway Publications failed to help, and the streamlined system, beginning with *Keypers* and *Maple Town* (September and October 1987), was not successful.

Television series proved to be almost the sole marketable content for comics. A smallish company, London Editions, was taken over by Egmont, rehoused in Manchester, and achieved its first big success with *My Little Pony* (5th September, 1985). This American television series made an empty-looking comic of large, poorly drawn pictures, but this seems to matter little to the small girls who buy the plastic toys so frequently featured in its sixteen simple pages. In fact, a companion comic had to be introduced to cater for the ever increasing demand, the monthly *My Little Pony and Friends* (February, 1987). The continual tying-in of comics to their American television programmes, which in turn are tied in with major toy manufacturers, has increasingly become a matter of concern. Apart from the moral question of the commercial links, there is the mass disappointment of youngsters when their favourite comics are suddenly cancelled as the television originals vanish to be replaced with new series based on new toys.

A final phenomenon of the eighties which looks like becoming the trend of the nineties is the flowering (if that is the right word) of the so-called Adult Comic. Small attempts had been made over the years as 'instant printing' and 'desktop publishing' became cheaper. At the end of the seventies, two brothers in the provinces put out 150 copies of their home made comic, *Viz* (December, 1979). By the end of the eighties, the national circulation of this bi-monthly comic (which still looks as if it is edited in the boys' bedroom) was touching one million! Despite its label, 'Not to be sold to persons under eighteen years of age', the humour of this comic is hardly adult, seeming to be firmly based on the number of rude and impolite words featured in each issue. Nevertheless, this humour is, it seems, what sells *Viz*, and many other publishers are currently seeking to share its success. Comics with names like *Smut* (13th May, 1989), *Gas* (29th September, 1989) and *Blag* (25th July, 1990) have proliferated, and even major companies like Fleetway (*Oink*, 3rd May 1986) and Marvel (*The Bog Paper*, 4th November, 1989) have slithered into the easy-money trap, nearly losing their shirts. Only D. C. Thomson have remained aloof, cheerfully celebrating the fiftieth anniversaries of *Dandy* (1987) and *Beano* (1988), Britain's oldest and still most popular comics.

THE ASSOCIATION OF COMICS ENTHUSIASTS: A. C. E.
Denis Gifford, the author of this book, is also the founder of the
Association of Comics Enthusiasts. Formed in 1978, A. C. E. is
still the only club for collectors of British comics. The annual
subscription of £8 brings you eight issues of the A. C. E. magazine,
Comic Cuts. Write to 80, Silverdale, Sydenham, SE26 4SJ.

Acknowledgements
All illustrations in this book are from comics in the author's
collection, with help from G. Newman, J. R. Swan, W. Westwater,
C. Wright, and Mrs G. M. Wilson. Grateful acknowledgement is
extended to the original publishers and the current copyright hold-
ers, I.P.C. Magazines Ltd. (Juveniles Division), L. Miller and Son
Ltd., D. C. Thomson and Co. Ltd., Walt Disney Productions Ltd.,
National Periodical Publications Inc., Magazine Management Co.
Inc. (Marvel Comics Group), Associated Newspapers Ltd., and
Fawcett Publications Inc.

*23. Beano Birthday! Fifty years old in July 1989, the 'Beano'
celebrated by bursting into full colour gravure — and raising its
price.*

INDEX OF TITLES

This index includes titles of comics mentioned in the text. A full chronological list of titles published since 1960 appears in the last two chapters of the book. Pages with illustrations are given in italics.

Ace Comics 29
Action Comics 32, *50*
Adventure 23
Adventures of Foxy
    Grandpa 28
All Fun 27
All Picture 19
All Star 27
Ally Sloper 6
Ally Sloper's Christmas
    Holidays 6
Ally Sloper's Half-
    Holiday 4, *5*, 6, 7, 8
Amazing Mystery Funnies
    32
American Humorist 27
Answers to
    Correspondents 7
Batman 49
Beano 24, *44*, 57, 69, *70*
Beezer 56
Best Budget 15
Big Budget *11*, 12, *13*, 28,
    35
Big Comic 15
Bobo Bunny 58
Bog Paper 69
Bo-Peep 17
Bouncer 22
Boy's Home Journal 12
Bubbles 17
Buddy 68
Bulldog Brittain 53
Bunty 57
Buster Brown 28
Butterfly 15, 19
Captain America 49, 58
Captain Marvel 49, *52*
Captain Miracle 53
Champion Comic 12
Cheerful 20
Chick's Own 17
Children's Fairy 17
Chips 8, *9*, 10, 11, 12, 14,
    15, 20, 23
Chuckler 21
Chuckles 15
Coloured Comic 14

Comet 54
Comic Adventures 27
Comic Bits 13
Comic Capers 27
Comic Cuts *3*, 7, 8, *9*, 10,
    11, 12, 14, *43*
Comic Home Journal 12
Comic Life 15
Comic Pictorial Nuggets
    10
Comic Pictorial Sheet 10
Comics, The 29
Comics Magazine 30
Comics on Parade 29
Cor 59
Cowboy Comics 57
Crackajack Funnies 29
Crackers 18, 27
Daily Express 57
Daily Mail 16, *42*
Daily Mirror 54, 58
Dandy 23, 24, *25*, 57, 69
Dan Leno's Comic Journal
    13
Dazzler 21
Detective Comics 49
Detective Picture Stories
    30
Dickory Dock 68
Dreamer 68
Eagle 55, *56*, 57, 58
Electroman 53
Extra Fun 50
Famous Funnies 29, 30,
    46, 55
Fantastic 58, 60
Fantastic Four 58
Favourite Comic 15
Feature Funnies 29, 32
Film Fun 8, 23, *24*, 26
Film Picture Stories 23
Firefly 17
Fitness and Sun 54
Flash 53
Flash Comics 50
Fresh Fun 50
Funnies, The 28, 29
Funny Cuts 10

Funny Folks 4, 7, 10, *34*
Funny Pages 30
Funny Picture Stories 30,
    31
Funny Wonder 11, 14, *17*
Gas 69
Girl 55
Girls' Crystal 55
Golden 18
Golden Penny 19, 20
Half Holiday 6
Halfpenny Comic 13
Happy Comic 20
Happy Days 18, *41*, 56
Harold Hare's Own Paper
    57
Harper's Weekly 8, 27
Holiday Comic 20
Hotspur 23
Huckleberry Hound
    Weekly 64
Illustrated Chips 8
Illustrated Tid-Bits 7
Jack and Jill 7, 56
Jack's Journal 7
Jack Simpleton *36*
Jester 15
Jingles 18
Joe 90 64
Joker 10, 20, *21*
Jolly Bits 11
Jolly Chuckles 52
Jolly Comic 18
Judge 7, 27
Judy (magazine) 4, 5, 8,
    10
Jumbo Comics 32
Jungle Jinks 18
Junior Express 57
Keen Detective Funnies
    32
Keypers 69
Kinema Comic 23
King Comics 29
Knock-out 8, 20, 26, 54,
    61
Lady Penelope 64
Larks 11, 15, 20

Laughter 7
Laurel and Hardy 59
Life 7, 27
Little Sparks 17
Lion 55, 56, 58
Lot-O-Fun 15
Magic 26
Man in the Moon 4
Maple Town 69
Marilyn 57
Marvelman 52, *53*
Merry and Bright 15, 19
Merry Midget 20
Merry Moments 19, 20
Merry Thoughts 15
Mickey Mouse Weekly 18, *40*, 57
Midget 20
Midget Comic 23
Mighty World of Marvel 64
Monster Comic 13, 19, 20
More Fun 29, 30
My Favourite 18
My Funnybone 15
My Little Pony 69
My Little Pony and Friends 69
New Adventure Comics 30
New Children's Encyclopaedia 15
New Comics 30
New Funnies *47*, 50
New Hotspur 57
New Triumph 27, 49
New York Herald 28, *37*
New York Journal 27
New York World 27
News of the World 55
Nikki 68
Nosey Parker's Midget Comic 23
Nuggets 10
Oink 69
Our Young Folks' Weekly Budget 10
Ovaltiney's Own Comic 22
Pepper Street 68
Pictorial Comic Life 13
Picture Fun 15

Picture Post 55
Picture Stories from the Bible 55
Playbox 16, 27
Playhour Pictures 56
Playtime 17, 23
Pow 57, *58*, 59
Puck 14, 15, 20, 28, *38*
Punch 4
Radio Fun 11, 13, 26, *45*, 56
Rainbow 15, *16*, *39*
Rattler 21
Rattler and Chuckler *22*
Return of the Jedi 64
Robin 55, 69
Rocket 22, 57
Rover 21, 23, 24
School Friend 55
Scraps 7, 10
Scream 68
Seaside Comic 20
Sensation Comics 49
Side-Splitters 12
Skipper 23
Skits 10
Slick Fun 50
Smash 57
Smiles 15
Smut 69
Snacks 7
Snapshots 10
South Wales Echo 54
Space Comics 53
Sparkler 18, 21
Sparks 17
Spiderman 57
Spider-Man Comics Weekly 64
Sports Fun 23
Spring Comic 20
Star Comics 32
Star Ranger 32
Star Wars 64
Story Nuggets 10
Summer Comic 20
Sun 54
Sunbeam 18
Sunday Fairy 17
Sunday Post 23
Sunny Comic 20
Sunshine 22

Super Comics 29
Super Duper 52
Super Star 52
Superman 49
Swift 55
Target 22
Teddy Tail 16
Terrific 58
Thrill Comics 50
Thunderbirds Specials 64
Tiger 56
Tiger Tim's Tales 16
Tiger Tim's Weekly 16
Tiny Tots 17
Tip Top 18
Tip Top Comic 20
Tip Top Comics 29
Tit Bits 7
Tom Browne's Annual 9
Top Spot 57
Topical Funnies 50, *51*
Topper 56
Tops 68
TV Century 21, 64
TV Comic 55
TV Express 57
TV Fan 56
TV Fun 56
TV Tops 68
TV Tornado 53
Up-To-Date Comics 20
Valiant 26
Varieties 11
Vault of Horror *48*, 55
Victory Funnies 54
Viz 69
Wags *32*
Walt Disney's Mickey Mouse 5, 17
War Comics 50
Western Picture Stories 30
Wham 57
Whiz Comics 49, 52
Whizzer and Chips 8, 54, 61
Wizard 23, 24
Wonder 11
Wonderman 53
World's Comic 10
Wow 30
Wow Comics 50
Zip 57